GOLDEN ROSARY EDITIONS

comprise oral teachings by
Khenchen Thrangu Rinpoche on the great
lineage masters of the Kagyu tradition.

They are reproduced through
the inspiration of H.H. Karmapa,
the blessing of Khenchen Thrangu Rinpoche,
and the guidance of Venerable Lama Karma Shedrup.

These editions are dedicated
to their long life and prosperity.

Zhyisil Chokyi Ghatsal Trust
Publications

£14·95

May this supreme, peerless teaching,

The precious treasure of the Victorious Ones

Spread and extend throughout the world,

Like the sun shining in the sky.

A Spiritual Biography *of* Marpa the Translator

by

Khabje Khenchen
Thrangu Rinpoche

ISBN Number: 1-877294-07-1

This publication is a joint venture between:

Namo Buddha Publications
P. O.Box 1083, Crestone,
CO 81131, USA
Email: cjohnson@ix.netcom.com
Thrangu Rinpoche's web site: www.rinpoche.com
and

Zhyisil Chokyi Ghatsal Trust Publications
PO Box 6259 Wellesley Street,
Auckland, New Zealand
Email: inquiries@greatliberation.org
Website: www.greatliberation.org

Acknowledgments
We would like to thank the persons who helped make this book possible. First of all, we would like to thank Ken and Katia Holmes for translating this work. We would also like to thank Margaret Neuman for transcribing the tapes and Jean Johnson for helping editing the manuscript. We would also like to thank Ani Migume of Gampo Abbey for transcribing a second biography of Marpa and Lama Yeshe Gyamtso for translating this teaching.

Notes
Technical words are italicized the first time that they appear to alert the reader that their definition can be found in the Glossary of Terms. The Tibetan words are given as they are pronounced, not spelled in Tibetan. We use B.C.E. (Before Current Era) for B.C. and C.E. (Current Era) for A.D.

Table of Contents

Ven. Lama Karma Shedrup Cho Gyi Senge Kartung

Foreword

The Golden Rosary Editions contain the spiritual biographies and teachings of the glorious Kagyupa lineage. The term "Golden Rosary" refers to this lineage of realized masters who have transmitted unbroken the profound Mahamudra teachings of the Lord Buddha to the present day. What makes these teachings so profound is that they contain instructions and practices which enable one to accomplish enlightenment in one lifetime.

One of the tremendous blessings of the Kagyu lineage is the diversity of lifestyles manifested by the lineage masters, showing that whatever our circumstances or lifestyle, we can practice these teachings and accomplish enlightenment. For example, Tilopa accomplished enlightenment while working as a menial labourer grounding sesame seeds. Others like Marpa were businessmen and had families. Marpa's student Milarepa was an ascetic who spent his life practicing in isolated caves, and one of his students, Gampopa, was a monk. Yet what they all had in common was that through practicing Mahamudra they all accomplished enlightenment. All this shows the great variety and power of the methods of Vajrayana for transforming one's mind through whatever circumstances. So similarly, if we practice Mahamudra with great diligence and effort we can achieve the fruition in one lifetime.

Therefore to read these spiritual biographies of the Kagyu lineage masters is a great inspiration to enter the path and they also provide encouragement and inspiration to continue when circumstances become difficult. In particular it is of great blessing to receive these teachings from Khenchen Thrangu Rinpoche, a master of great wisdom and compassion. Because he has directly realised Mahamudra and is a holder of this lineage he can transmit not only the words but the meaning.

So, I encourage all students to read these spiritual biographies and pray that it will inspire you to fulfil all the aspirations of the lineage masters. And may this merit cause the life and teachings of the great masters to flourish and remain for many eons benefiting limitless sentient beings.

Zhyisil Chokyi Ghatsal Trust
3/1 Franklin Rd, Ponsonby
Auckland, NZ

Biography
of Thrangu Rinpoche (b. 1933)

The lineage of the Thrangu Rinpoche incarnations began in the fifteenth century when the Seventh Karmapa, Chodrak Gyatso visited the region of Thrangu in Tibet. At this time His Holiness Karmapa established Thrangu Monastery and enthroned Sherap Gyaltsen as the first Thrangu Rinpoche, recognizing him as the re-established emanation of Shuwu Palgyi Senge, one of the twenty-five great siddha disciples of Guru Padmasambhava.

Khenchen Thrangu Rinpoche is the ninth incarnation of this lineage and was born in Kham, Tibet in 1933. When he was four, H.H. the Sixteenth Gyalwa Karmapa and Palpung Situ Rinpoche recognized him as the incarnation of Thrangu Tulku by prophesying the names of his parents and the place of his birth.

He entered Thrangu monastery and from the ages of seven to sixteen he studied reading, writing, grammar, poetry, and astrology, memorised ritual texts, and completed two preliminary retreats. At sixteen under the direction of Khenpo Lodro Rabsel he began the study of the three vehicles of Buddhism while staying in retreat.

At twenty-three he received full ordination from the Karmapa. When he was twenty-seven Rinpoche left Tibet for India at the time of the Communist invasion. He was called to Rumtek, Sikkim, where the Karmapa had his seat in exile. At thirty-five he took the geshe examination before 1500 monks at Buxador monastic refugee camp in Bengal India and was awarded the degree of Geshe Lharampa. On his return to Rumtek he was named Abbot of Rumtek monastery and the Nalanda Institute for Higher Buddhist studies at Rumtek. He has been the personal teacher of the four principal Karma Kagyu tulkus: Shamar Rinpoche, Situ Rinpoche, Jamgon Kongtrul Rinpoche and Gyaltsab Rinpoche.

Thrangu Rinpoche has travelled extensively throughout Europe, the Far East and the USA. He is the abbot of Gampo Abbey, Nova Scotia, and of Thrangu House, Oxford, in the UK. In 1984 he spent several months in Tibet where he ordained over 100 monks and nuns and visited several monasteries. He has also founded Thrangu Tashi Choling monastery in Boudhnath; a retreat centre and college at Namo Buddha east of the Katmandu Valley, and has established a school in Boudhnath for the general education of lay children and young monks. He also built Tara Abbey in Katmandu. In October of 1999 he consecrated the college at Sarnath which will accept students from the different traditions of Buddhism and will be open to western students as well.

Thrangu Rinpoche, a recognised master of Mahamudra meditation has given teachings in over 25 countries. He is especially known for taking complex teachings and making them accessible to western students.

More recently, because of his vast knowledge of the Dharma, he was appointed by His Holiness the Dalai Lama to be the personal tutor for the Seventeenth Karmapa Urgyen Trinley Dorje.

Preface

This book is part of a series on the great lineage masters of the Kagyu lineage. This lineage of Tibetan Buddhism was founded by Tilopa who was born about 1,000 years ago. Tilopa was an extremely accomplished master and passed the tantric Buddhist teachings to Naropa. All this happened in India in the eleventh century C.E. In Naropa's lifetime the courageous Marpa came from the mysterious country of Tibet to receive these teachings and propagate them throughout Tibet. This was fortuitous because in the next two centuries, Buddhism was to be almost completely obliterated from the Indian subcontinent.

The teachings that Marpa received and then gave to his disciples have been passed down without distortion to the Venerable Thrangu Rinpoche. Thrangu Rinpoche has been recognized as an outstanding teacher. He has practiced these teachings so that when he teaches about Marpa he conveys not only the words of the teaching, but also their meaning.

Thrangu Rinpoche has traveled around the world many times, visiting now over 30 countries both East and West. In these travels he has taught almost non-stop for a decade, stopping usually for less than two weeks at a single center. In this unceasing teaching, he has emphasized again and again, that when beginning to practice one must develop the right view by studying the dharma teachings with a complete and open mind. Not only has he emphasized developing the correct view, but he has encouraged all students to find an appropriate guru and actually practice the Buddhist teachings. This is not an easy path and the student may encounter discouraging times when he or she doesn't feel like practicing any more. At these times Thrangu Rinpoche has suggested that students should read the spiritual biographies of the great Buddhist masters to gain encouragement to continue to practice.

It is in this light that Namo Buddha and Zhyisil Chokyi Ghatsal Publications feel fortunate to offer this spiritual biography of Marpa.

Thrangu Rinpoche actually gave teachings on Marpa on two different occasions – once at Samye Ling in the early 1980s which was translated by Ken and Katia Holmes. The second set of teachings was given at Halifax in 1992 with Lama Yeshe Gyamtso translating. Since Rinpoche emphasized different aspects of Marpa's life, these two teachings have been combined to make this book.

Clark Johnson, Ph.D.

"Marpa"

Calligraphy by Khenchen Thrangu Rinpoche

1

The Life of Marpa

There are three Tibetan forefathers of the Kagyu lineage: Marpa, Milarepa, and Gampopa. Marpa (1012-1097 C.E.) was seminal to the lineage because he actually brought the teachings from India to Tibet. Marpa had tremendous courage and determination; he didn't consider the risks or difficulties involved in going to India to obtain the Buddhist teachings. He didn't do it to become rich or famous or to achieve happiness. He did it to establish the pure Buddhist teachings in Tibet.

There were two great waves of transmissions of the *dharma* into Tibet: the "early period of translations" (Tib. *tan pa nga dar*),[1] in which a few great sponsors supported these works of translation; and the later wave, called "the later period of translation" (Tib. *tan pa phyi dar*), in which there weren't any sponsors. Being part of this second wave, Marpa had to rely entirely on his own motivation and determination to bring the teachings to Tibet. It was through his work that the teachings took root in Tibet and enabled many people to practice the teachings and thereby attain liberation.

The subject of this book is the life of Marpa the Translator. It is very important to understand Marpa's life because he is a special example within the tradition of the Kagyu lineage. A complete account of Marpa's life can be found in *The Life of Marpa the Translator* by Tsang Nyön Heruka.[2]

This present book constitutes a different kind of biography and is based on another account of Marpa's life called, *The Life of Marpa the Translator: Seeing Accomplishes All.*[3] (refer to pg. 91 for author details.)

Here I would like to make a few observations.

In Tibet, this type of biography is called a *"namtar,"* which literally means "full liberation." The reason a biography is called a *namtar* is that it depicts the obstacles and impediments that lamas encountered at the beginning of their path, and how, in practicing the dharma and relying on their guru, the obstacles were overcome. These religious biographies describe how lamas were able to achieve complete liberation and how in doing so they were able to greatly benefit others through their teaching. These biographies were not written simply to promote the reputation of the lineage lamas. Rather, they describe the circumstances in which these teachers began, and how, within the limitations of their beginning, they were able to practice and attain liberation. The special function of a *namtar* is as a "spiritual" biography. It is written to encourage us by showing us how these practitioners dealt with their particular situations.

Marpa did not become a monk like Shariputra,[4] for example. He was also quite angry and arrogant, and was, in the early part of his life, an extremely selfish person. Yet at the same time he had the tremendous courage to achieve *enlightenment* himself and to help others. He was extremely intelligent and very diligent, and he had a great deal of faith and confidence in – and devotion to – the dharma. He also developed genuine love and compassion for other beings.

The process that Marpa underwent during his training transformed his defects, such as arrogance, into good qualities such as courage that could benefit others. By this process, the qualities themselves expanded so that by the end of his training they actually became his experience and realization of completeness. He had become a supreme *siddha* (i.e. an enlightened being). This expansion of Marpa's example and teaching continue in the extraordinary instructions that we practice to this very day in and through the unbroken Kagyu lineage.

Marpa developed an extraordinary compassion that was not *idiot compassion* or *partial compassion*. It was intelligent compassion, meaning that it was not limited by sentiment or scope. He did not focus his compassion only towards his family or the people living in his neighborhood, but extended it to all those who would practice the *Vajrayana* in the future. To make the practice possible for future generations, he engaged in acts of great hardship. Specifically, he went to India three times to receive teachings and bring them back so that people could practice these teachings in the future.

A Prayer to Marpa

The life of the great master Marpa in a very condensed form can be described in three stages. These can be found in the prayer, *The All-Accomplishing Melody*, composed by Khyentse Rinpoche. The prayer describes the life story of Marpa in three verses.

The first line says:

Through his great determination and courage, he traveled many times to the holy land.

The Holy Land refers to India. It was through Marpa's great courage and determination, his profound devotion and his incredible compassion for all disciples (present and future) that he was able to overcome the difficulties and hardships of three journeys to India. The first verse focuses us on these qualities.

The second line tells us:

With great intelligence he saw the essential nature of all things.

This verse refers to the quality of the very sharp intelligence of Marpa. It identifies intelligence as proceeding from the courage, devotion and compassion of the first verse, and then generating insight. Since Marpa clearly saw the teachings of the Buddha, particularly the Vajrayana teachings, he was able to secure even the essence of the very deep *tantras* to bring with him to Tibet. Among the tantras, he particularly concentrated on bringing the highest tantra, the *Anuttarayoga,* to Tibet. He realized the meaning of these tantras and assimilated them completely. Not only did he understand them, but he used them all the time, tasting the flavor of the teachings completely. These teachings became a source of constant and direct experience for him, and that is why it is said that it was with great intelligence that he could see the true nature of phenomena.[5]

The third line says:

Through great realization, he manifested many kinds of miracles.

What is meant by doing miracles? There are miracles that can be done physically, verbally, and mentally. Physical miracles are used to arouse faith in the minds of people who do not have faith. Miracles of speech occur when teachings and instructions automatically generate realization in the disciple, without *skillful means.* Through the lama's words, disciples may achieve as high a level of realization as the lama. Through the miraculous power of the lama's speech, ordinary people are able to immediately assimilate the instructions so that they can accomplish the purification of impurities, in particular the *disturbing emotions* (Skt. *kleshas*).[6] When this occurs in the disciple as a fully developed realization and understanding, it is a miracle of mind.

How can a lama transmit this power of realization to others through speech? It is because the lama possesses very great qualities him or herself. The lama has the qualities of great compassion, diligence, courage, and determination. It is these qualities that give the lama the miraculous power to transfer realization to others. The third line refers to Marpa's capacity to perform miracles of body, speech, and mind. These manifestations referred to in the prayer are described in more detail in the biography of Marpa.

This biography of Marpa, *The Life of Marpa the Translator: Seeing Accomplishes All,* has five chapters. The first describes the events from Marpa's birth to when he encounters the dharma. The next three chapters describe his dharma activity, which corresponds to the three lines just given. The last chapter of the biography describes his passing away.

Marpa's Early Life

Marpa was born in Tibet, in the central province, called "U," which simply means "central province." There are three main areas in Tibet: U, Sang in the west and Kham in the east. Marpa, the youngest of three sons, was born in the south of U in a place called Lhotrak.

When we read the life stories of great masters, it can be rather discouraging. We find examples of people who by nature seem very peaceful, kind, good, and disciplined. We feel that we can't compare with them because we are angry and agitated by many disturbing emotions. We expect a great master to achieve great things; not ordinary people like ourselves. Yet the great masters teach us that if we practice the dharma, then little by little, we can learn to pacify, train and discipline the mind through meditation.

Marpa's life relates quite a different story. Marpa was a very angry person. He engaged in many worldly activities. He lived as an ordinary householder, had a farm, a wife, and many children. But through his tremendous determination and courage he managed to practice the dharma and achieve realization.

As a child he was temperamental and quick to anger. Due to his terrible temper, his family thought that something needed to be done to make him more manageable. His father thought that if they made him become a monk, he might become more peaceful and self-controlled. So his father and mother decided to make him follow a religious path. At that time there was a lama by the name of Drogmi Lotsawa (*lotsawa* is Tibetan for "translator"), who had been to India and brought back many texts and done many translations. He was recognized in Tibet as a very good and special teacher.

So Marpa was sent to Drogmi Lotsawa. When they met, Marpa asked for *empowerments* and instructions. But Drogmi didn't really give him very many empowerments. However, under Drogmi's instruction Marpa learned the main dialect of India and became quite proficient in this language. Without a strong karmic tie to Drogmi, Marpa began developing a strong desire to go to India himself, rather than staying and learning from Drogmi.

In those days there were many translators in Tibet. Many were great scholars who benefited the dharma, but generally they were interested in translating texts on the arts and sciences, such as astrology, Sanskrit medicine, and so forth. These were, of course, helpful to the dharma student, but not as helpful as what Marpa would translate because there were few scholars who were translating Vajrayana texts from Sanskrit into Tibetan. Marpa's translations were to become distinguished by the fact that the texts that he received and translated were previously unknown and unavailable to the Tibetan practitioner. Unknown were such texts as the explanations of the *creation stage* and *completion stage* of the *Guhyasamaja* and the *Hevajra* tantras, or the teachings connected to the *dharma protectors*. Marpa relied upon the Sanskrit documents of teachers that no one in Tibet had ever heard of, and it was from these teachers that he received and translated teachings that no one had ever received before. The result of his work is that today, more than a millennium later, there is an unbroken lineage to these teachings, the Kagyu linage.

Marpa Goes to India

The second chapter of the original text describes how Marpa went to India three times. The journey from Tibet to India was not like traveling under modern conditions. It was an incredibly difficult and arduous journey. The roads were very poor and it was always possible to encounter wild animals on the road. On the Tibetan part of the journey, one had to cross very high passes and endure extreme cold. Closer to India, the passage was through incredibly hot jungles with many diseases, parasites, and poisonous snakes. One had to ford very wild rivers and the danger of encountering robbers, who could easily kill you, was constant.

Marpa didn't consider any of these difficulties at all. He went on this journey, not once, but three times. He was able to do this entirely because of his great courage and determination. His courage came from his tremendous devotion to the dharma. He had great faith in the teachings and what gave him his determination was his great compassion for others who would need the teachings.

Marpa's First Journey

When Marpa wanted to go to India the first time, he went to see his parents and said, "I've decided to go to India. Would you kindly give me my share of the inheritance so I can convert it into gold and take it with me to India." His parents and brothers tried to dissuade him saying, "There isn't really any point in going to India. We don't see why you should go there and become a translator. If you want to practice the dharma, why not stay here and do it in Tibet? Also, if you can't practice, then why not become a farmer and do something useful?" So they argued and argued and tried to talk Marpa out of going to India, but nothing worked. Marpa had an unflinching resolve to go and that was that.

There were two other Tibetans from the same area where Marpa lived who were to travel with Marpa to India. But in the end their families talked them out of going. So Marpa finally left on his own. When Marpa was quite far from home, he met up with someone else who was traveling to India, Nyö Lotsawa, and they started traveling together on the way to India through Nepal.

On this first journey to India, Marpa was to stay in Nepal for three years. The change in temperature and humidity from Tibet to India was unbearable for Tibetans unless they gradually acclimatized themselves to it. So Marpa remained in Nepal for three years, studying more Sanskrit, learning other Indian languages, and getting used to the climate. But in addition, Marpa had many valuable experiences.

On the first day of their arrival in Nepal[7] they came upon a whole crowd of people and they were told, "If you want to get yourself a little bit of food and drink, just go where there's a crowd." Marpa asked, "But what's going on here?" People answered, "Today there are two disciples of Naropa from Pontengpa who have come here to give teachings."

Just hearing the name of Naropa triggered something very strong inside Marpa. It awoke his subconscious memory. In his past lives he had a connection with Naropa. Marpa immediately felt tremendous faith and devotion. He had a very strong urge to go to where Naropa's disciples were teaching. He said to his friend Nyö Lotsawa, "Let's go there and receive teachings and find out what is going on."

Two lamas named Chitherpa and Paindapa from Pontengpa were there to give teachings on the Guhyasamaja tantra. Some of the Nepalese saw Marpa and Nyö Lotsawa and said, "Here come the Tibetans. We won't be receiving any profound teachings or empowerments today because Tibetans are rather stupid. They are like cows and won't understand the language or anything. What a bother that they came." But Nyö Lotsawa knew Nepalese and he became very hurt and upset at being called a cow. At the teachings, he turned his back to the lamas and recited *mantras* all the way through, which was very disrespectful.

The next day, Marpa said, "Let's go back and receive some more teachings." But Nyö Lotsawa said, "No, I'm not going to bother. They said we were cows, so I'm not going to bother if I'm a cow." Marpa went back alone and, in fact, received many teachings and empowerments. After the teachings Marpa went up to these two students of Naropa. He wanted to know of good teachers who could be found in India and he wanted to talk about Naropa. He felt a very great urge to know more about him. The two lamas told him about Naropa's special qualities, which kindled Marpa's desire to go and see this great lama even more. Marpa felt an inner calling to see Naropa and decided to ignore the advice of the lamas, who said, "Maybe you should stay here to accustom yourself to the heat, and once you've been in Nepal a while, then you can travel to India." But the call of karma[8] was so strong that Marpa decided to go to find Naropa in India as soon as possible.

Marpa left with his companion Nyö Lotsawa and they made the difficult and arduous journey, eventually arriving in India. From all the conversations with the Nepalese and with the lamas he met in India, Marpa knew that he wanted to meet that very great *pandita* and realized-being Naropa. He said to Nyö Lotsawa, "You know that everyone says he is the greatest, so why don't we go and see him?" However, Nyö Lotsawa didn't have any particular connection with Naropa from his past lives, so he said, "Oh, I've heard good things about Naropa. But you know what happened to his teacher Tilopa, he went really wild and is living like a wild yogi. Naropa is turning into the same thing and I'm not keen on that. Besides in India you can find very great teachers and panditas all over the place. So I don't think I have any particular desire to go find Naropa. I can meet good teachers anywhere." So they decided that each would go his own way and find his own lamas.

Eventually, Marpa was able to meet Naropa. Naropa, with joy, declared, "You are the one predicted by my own teacher (Tilopa) and I name you 'Marpa, The Intelligence of Dharma' (Marpa Chokyi Lodro). In the future you will bring the Buddha's teachings to Tibet."

Naropa, being very, very happy to meet Marpa, looked after him and treated him very kindly. First he gave Marpa the three tantric teachings connected with the Hevajra tantra: the Tatnig tantra, the *spiritual songs* (Skt. *dohas*) and the Samputa tantra.

Marpa spent about a year studying and learning these three tantras. When the year was over, Marpa took a break and went to the neighboring town where he ran into Nyö Lotsawa. They quite naturally talked about what they had been doing since parting ways. Nyö Lotsawa asked, "What did you study?" and Marpa replied that he had studied the Hevajra tantras. They talked quite a lot about the Hevajra teachings and Marpa realized that he understood more than his friend did. But then Nyö Lotsawa told him that the Hevajra tantra was already being practiced in Tibet and since it was already there, they should really try to learn the Guhyasamaja tantra, which is part of the collection called the *"father tantras."*[9] Nyö Lotsawa said, "If you know how to practice this tantra, then you can gain complete control over all the energies in your body, to the extent that you can bring all the subtle energies of your body to the tip of your fingers.[10] Having done that you will have reached *Buddhahood*, then you can go back to where you were," meaning that this tantra leads to easy realization.

As Nyö went on and on talking about the Guhyasamaja teachings, Marpa realized that he didn't know anything about these teachings. He went straight back to Naropa and told him what had happened and begged to receive this teaching as quickly as possible.

When Naropa heard his request, he said that the greatest teacher of the Guhyasamaja teaching was Yeshe Nyingpo (Skt. *Jnanagharba*) who lived in western India and that Marpa should go to him to request the teachings. He then told Marpa that he wouldn't meet any difficulties on the way, but that when he got there he should work very hard to master this practice. So Marpa visited Yeshe Nyingpo and was able to receive the empowerments and all the instructions on the Guhyasamaja tantra. He also received from Yeshe Nyingpo the empowerments and instructions to the *Kriya tantra* and the *Yoga tantra*.

On Marpa's return to Naropa he stopped at a temple on the road and met Nyö Lotsawa again. The two friends started talking about their studies and Nyö Lotsawa asked, "What have you been doing lately?" They began discussing this father tantra of Guhyasamaja and again Marpa knew all the teachings more thoroughly than Nyö Lotsawa. Then Nyö Lotsawa said, "Oh well, that's really good. But you know the Guhyasamaja teachings are already known in Tibet. What we really need in Tibet is something from the *mother tantras* called the *Mahamaya* practice, which we don't have in Tibet. This is a teaching that talks about the static aspect of the *subtle channels* located in the body, and the dynamic aspect of the subtle energies that circulate in the body, and how *bodhichitta* is within the whole system. These are very profound instructions and this is what we should try to bring to Tibet."

Then, of course, Marpa realized that he didn't know anything about the Mahamaya teachings. When he returned to Naropa and Naropa asked, "Well, how did it go. Did you get the Guhyasamaja teachings from Lama Yeshe Nyingpo?" Marpa answered, "Yes, I indeed received all these wonderful teachings. Everything went very well until I met my friend on the way and he told me that we really need to take the Mahamaya teachings to Tibet. So please give these to me."

Naropa had sent Marpa to study the Guhyasamaja with another teacher because he wanted Marpa to get that particular line of blessing from that teacher. Naropa could have given the teachings himself, but he wanted Marpa to have that particular transmission. He thought that later on he could always give other transmissions to Marpa if need be. Concerning the Mahamaya teachings, he said to Marpa, "Well, the one who is really the master of this teaching is Kukkuripa who lives on an island in a lake of poison. He is really the master of the mother tantra, so you must go and see him to receive this teaching."

Before leaving to go south to see Kukkuripa, Marpa went with Naropa to a cemetery where several *yogis* were living. Naropa pointed his finger at them and said, "Marpa is going to receive teachings from the teacher who lives on an island in a lake of poison. I want you to protect him from all dangers on his journey." One of the yogis stepped forward and said, "I promise to protect him from poisonous snakes" while another said, "I promise to protect him from wild animals" while the third said, "I promise to protect him from all the evil influences that come from non-human beings." Then just before Marpa left, Naropa advised him that when he arrived, he would find the *mahasiddha* Kukkuripa and warned him that Kukkuripa would look quite strange, all covered with hair, looking almost like a monkey with the lower part of his body being a rather horrible color. And he said, "Don't be surprised because he often shows himself in all kinds of strange forms. So when you arrive there, don't have any doubts. Think that he is the guru that you are looking for and ask him for the Mahamaya teaching and tell him you were sent by your guru." Then Naropa gave him a letter to give to the teacher when he arrived.

On the way Marpa encountered many hardships and difficulties. But he prayed to Naropa with great faith and somehow managed to deal with all these troubles. Finally when he arrived on the island, he saw somebody sitting against a tree with hair covering his whole body, not saying a word. Marpa said, "Hello, who is there? Is that Kukkuripa?" Then Kukkuripa said, "What's that, a flat-nosed man?" (meaning a Tibetan who has Mongolian features). "Where do you come from, flat-nose? Why did you take all the trouble to come here? Who are you looking for anyway? I've never heard of Kukkuripa and I've never seen him." Marpa was taken aback, but he couldn't see any other person there, so he decided that this hairy person must really be Kukkuripa. As instructed by Naropa, he went up to the weird creature and said, "I've been sent by the great pandita Naropa, my guru, to ask you to give me the Mahamaya teachings, so please give them to me" and he gave him the letter from Naropa. Kukkuripa then replied, "Great pandita Naropa? What are you talking about? He's a joke of a pandita. You make me laugh. He doesn't know anything. He has no experience of meditation. As for the teaching of Mahamaya, just ask him to give it to you. But leave me alone. Why did you come and disturb me anyway? Just go and see your joke of a pandita and ask him for the teaching."

After Kukkuripa said this and a lot of other terrible things about Naropa, he later confessed and said, "No, in fact, Naropa is a tremendous teacher. He is a great *mahapandita* and a realized being. And, of course, he could give you the Mahamaya teachings, but since I have a special transmission of this teaching he sent you to me." Then he gave Marpa the complete transmission of the Mahamaya teaching.

What Marpa Studied

The Vajrayana basically consists of two aspects: one is the aspect of means (Skt. *upaya*), which emphasizes a stage of practice called the creation stage; the other is the aspect of knowledge or insight (Skt. *prajna*), which emphasizes the completion stage. The tantras can be divided according to whether their emphasis is on means or knowledge. The tantras emphasizing means or method are called the "father tantras" and those emphasizing knowledge are called the "mother tantras."

What Marpa initially received from Naropa was the instruction in the mother tantra, particularly the most profound of the "mother tantras" known as the Hevajra tantra. He received the empowerments and the instructions for practice as well as the transmission and explanation of the original teaching of this practice given by the Buddha, called the "root tantra." The explanatory tantra that goes with the Hevajra tantra together with Naropa's explanation is now called the "two examinations" and the explanatory tantra is called the "vajra tent" or the "dakini vajra tantra." Marpa received this tradition of Hevajra in its entirety.

Then he requested instruction in the "father tantra." He asked Naropa for teachings of the most essential father tantra called the "Guhyasamaja." Naropa said that it would be better if he received this from the pandita Jnanagarbha, who used this tantra in his own practice and had received a special tradition of it. Marpa received the Guhyasamaja from Jnanagarbha as well as another mother tantra. In one of his spiritual songs Marpa says, "I received the most profound of mother tantras, Hevajra, and its essence, Mahamaya." Marpa was referring to the Mahamaya tantra as the essence of the mother tantra that he had received from Kukkuripa.

All these teachings of Hevajra, Guhyasamaja and Mahamaya that Marpa received on his first journey to India were the extremely profound instructions of the highest Anuttarayoga tantra. Marpa received what was called the "uncommon transmission," containing the two aspects of practice: the path of liberation, also called the path of Mahamudra; and the path of means, also called the *"Six Yogas of Naropa."*[11] The path of liberation became the main meditation practice of the Kagyu lineage and Marpa received this from Maitripa, who was to become another of Marpa's main Indian teachers, in accordance with a prophecy by Naropa. While Marpa was receiving the extensive instruction in *Mahamudra* from Maitripa, he also received instruction in a tantra called *"Praises Sung as Song."* Further, he received transmissions for the spiritual songs of the siddhas such as Saraha, Shavari and so forth.

First, Marpa received these numerous instructions then he actually put them into practice through meditation. Having gained experience of these instructions in meditation, he then investigated them further by cutting through all his doubts and hesitations about the teachings.

2

Marpa Meets Maitripa

*T*he next teacher that Marpa met in India was the great Vajrayana master, Maitripa. From Maitripa, Marpa received the Mahamudra instructions. Marpa had already received Mahamudra instructions from Naropa, so we may wonder why he wanted to receive them a second time. He did this because Naropa and Maitripa represented two different streams of transmission of the Mahamudra teachings. Naropa had what is called the "short transmission" because he received these teachings directly from Tilopa, who received them directly from *Vajradhara*.[12] Maitripa had what was called the "longer transmission" because he received these teachings from Shavari who received them from Nagarjuna, who received them from the mahasiddha Saraha. So Marpa received two streams of transmission: the short (or near) one, and the longer one.

Maitripa was staying in a monastery in a very isolated place called the "Mountain that Looked like Blazing Fire." The road to it was extremely difficult to travel so Marpa met with tremendous difficulties on the way. Some people he met on the way told him, "You'd better give up because you'll never get there alive." But Marpa answered, "I'm not going there to have a good time. I'm also not going to become rich or famous. I'm going there to find the precious dharma teachings and even if I die on the way, then I will know that it was for the right purpose." So without hesitation Marpa just carried on and finally reached Maitripa.

When Marpa met Maitripa, he requested the Mahamudra instructions, which Maitripa, out of his great compassion, gave him. These were the teachings Maitrepa had received from the lineage of Saraha. Maitripa then gave these instructions to Marpa, notably the instructions on the realization of the true nature of mind.

In addition to the Mahamudra teachings that Maitripa had received, Maitripa gave Marpa the teachings on two more tantras. These were the *Chanting the Names of Manjushri*[13] tantra, which concerns Mahamudra, and the tantra commentary on the Mahamudra by the Buddha. In addition to this he gave Marpa the *Spiritual Songs of Saraha*.[14] These are beautifully inspired spiritual songs in which Saraha gives instruction on how to gain realization of the true nature of mind. By receiving all of these instructions Marpa was able to eliminate all doubts and misunderstandings concerning the Mahamudra so that he understood the Mahamudra just as it was.

After receiving the instructions from Maitripa, Maitripa sang Marpa the *Song of Twelve Instructions,* which is discussed in the next chapter. Marpa returned to Naropa, who then sent him to the funeral ground of Sosadvipa to receive teachings from the wisdom *dakini,* called "the one with the bone ornaments."[15] Naropa told Marpa to receive the empowerment and instructions of Catuhpitha (Tib. *Dorje Dentze*) from her. After he had received these, he had received five main teachings in all: the Hevajra, the Guhyasamaja, the Mahamaya, the remote transmission of the Mahamudra from Maitripa, and now the teachings and instructions on Dorje Dentze. One might note that these five teachings were given to Marpa in the "usual manner," which means that although they were very, very profound teachings, there was nothing really exceptional about the way in which the teachings were given or received.

Teachings from Naropa

Marpa also received very special teachings and transmissions from Naropa such as the teachings of *Chakrasamvara* as discussed in *The*

Rain of Wisdom.[16] When Naropa gave Marpa the Chakrasamvara empowerment and instructions, he sang a spiritual song distilling this moment. Then Marpa replied in kind with another spontaneous spiritual song, to Naropa, requesting the full cycle of instructions on Chakrasamvara, including the empowerment, the actual tantric teaching, the commentary on the teaching, and all the meditation instructions connected with this practice. In answer to this request, Naropa gave him the full empowerment with extremely detailed teachings on the tantra, as well as the commentary on the tantra. All of these teachings strongly emphasized the practice aspect. Then Naropa gave the four transmissions he had received from Tilopa, which are also called the "Six Yogas of Naropa."

Finally and importantly, Naropa gave Marpa the Mahamudra instructions, in which he described Mahamudra in terms of the "naturalness" of mind. This means that when we meditate, we are not trying to develop a new mind that we didn't have before or to create a new mind with all new qualities. The purpose of meditation is not to change our old mind into a new one, or even to eliminate whatever we had before, but to leave the mind just as it was initially. This "naturalness" is the same as the innate intelligence that is already within the mind. The Mahamudra instructions of Naropa teach us to recognize this natural state of the mind.

With all of these instructions, Marpa then meditated and practiced and achieved full realization. In particular, Marpa mastered the practice of "*subtle heat*" (*tummo,* in Tibetan). In tummo practice Marpa gained the constant and simultaneous experience of great bliss, clarity and non-thought, which result in the highest level of realization. In this way Marpa became extremely accomplished and developed many positive qualities. For instance, when he sat down to meditate, he was able to do so for seven days without moving. He was in such a state that whether it was day or night, he was constantly immersed in a state of great joy. When he got to this point of constant meditation, he remembered the twelve years that he had spent in India and Nepal. He realized the great number of teachings, tantras, commentaries and instructions he had mastered. He saw that he had mastered not only a literal understanding of the words but a full understanding of the meaning of these teachings. He had found what he wanted to achieve through practice. He had gotten to the point that he couldn't have any regrets about anything that had happened during these twelve years because he had fully satisfied his search for teaching and realization. He now felt he didn't need to look to anyone else to improve his meditation or to teach others.

At the same time as his achievement was complete, his provision of gold was exhausted. It was time to return to Tibet, to give to his Tibetan students all the teachings that he had received from Naropa and Maitripa, and to get more gold to return to India to complete any missing teachings. His greatest wish was for these teachings to spread and flourish in Tibet.

Marpa assembled all his companions and fellow disciples who were studying with Naropa and told them to prepare for a celebration and a feast before he went. Whatever bits of gold were left were put together to make an offering to Naropa. They had this last party with all the dharma friends and the guru. Marpa reflected on how he had come to India and was able to meet the finest mahasiddhas and thus receive all the teachings of the Buddha, the great tantras and their commentaries. As a proficient translator of Sanskrit he was also able to make the teachings available so that their real meaning could be discovered. He had been lucky not to have any troubles with his health or any great injury. So he said, "Today, I feel a joy like I've never known before. And now it is time to go back to Tibet."

Then Marpa composed a spiritual song for Naropa:

Naropa, you are a very fortunate person because through the amazing amount of virtue you must have gathered in other lives, you were able to receive the direct teachings of Tilopa. Then you had the courage to go through twelve very difficult ordeals.[17] Then in one instant, you were able to realize the true nature of everything. So you are truly a wonderful being, a great mahasiddha.

As for me, I am only a petty translator from Tibet. But still I'm fortunate enough to have the good karma not just to meet you, but also to receive great teachings from you. I received the Hevajra teaching, the Mahamaya teachings and particularly the teaching that is like the essence of all the others, the Chakrasamvara teaching.

Marpa continued his spiritual song:

Through untainted meditation, I have been able to meditate without moving for seven days. I have gained an understanding of the prana, this very subtle energy that is carried by the subtle airs in the body. Because this prana has become very pure, it doesn't circulate just through my right and left channels, but now goes directly through the central channel. It is like going through space itself. And because of this, I now experience the great bliss, the great clarity, and the great non-thought of mind. Also, now all illusions of the mind dissolve naturally into the dharmakaya and all outer appearances are just like conjured illusions that disappear within Mahamudra.

When I recognized the true nature of my mind, it was like finding a very, very old friend that I haven't seen for a long time. Having realized my own mind, when I have experiences, the experiences are completely ineffable, beyond anything I could express, anything I could even imagine. It is like the experience of a mute who is having a dream, but can never tell anyone about the dream because he cannot speak.

Through whose kindness did I get all this? It was through your kindness, Naropa. I hope that you may still look after me with such great kindness in the future.

In answer to Marpa's spiritual song, Naropa replied in a very short song of advice:

Marpa, you should never allow yourself to be dominated by the eight worldly concerns.

You should never let your mind think in terms of subject and object, of "I" and "other."

You should never put other people down or criticize them in an aggressive way.

But you should always study and reflect as much as you can, because this will act like a lamp to remove all darkness. This study and reflection is the path that leads to liberation, so always maintain your studies.

And as for your relationship to the guru, so far you have relied very closely on your guru and you have respected him and served him well. And as you did before, so should you always do in the future. Always rely on your guru.

Then Naropa concluded his spiritual song with these words:

Never forget that your mind is like a jewel. It is a jewel because it is the source of all happiness and all goodness. Know that what I have told you is in your mind and never forget it. Never leave this knowledge unused. Always use it; always be aware of it.

Having received all this advice, Marpa took his leave from Naropa and promised that he would come back to India one more time.

Marpa's Return to Tibet

By the end of his first journey to India, Marpa had been in India and Nepal for twelve years. He had mastered Sanskrit and several other Indian and Nepali languages. He had received the empowerments, transmissions, and instructions for a variety of tantras. He not only studied these teachings, he also practiced them. Not only did he practice them, he developed signs of real accomplishment such as the ability to develop subtle inner heat in his tummo meditation.

Pleased with his accomplishments, Marpa returned to Tibet on the same route through Nepal that he had taken to go to India.

3

The Song of the Twelve Instructions

*D*uring the first journey and before his return to Naropa, Maitripa gave Marpa one last instruction, in the form of a spiritual song. In twelve verses this song embodied all the *key instructions* of Mahamudra meditation. These verses are called the "Twelve Points of Instruction" and when Marpa heard them, he immediately realized how beneficial the instructions had been for him and felt a great affinity for these teachings.

The first verse of the song consists of two lines:

1. O son, if the root of faith is not firm the root of non-duality will not be firm.

The first point is that the root of all practice is faith and this faith must be very firm and stable. If this faith is not strong, then everything else that comes out of the practice will be weak. So faith is the root of practice. To use an analogy: if the root of a tree is weak, then the trunk and branches and leaves will not be strong. It is said that faith is the root of the understanding of *emptiness*[18] (Skt. *shunyata*) and that faith is the understanding of non-dual nature. If our faith is not strong, we cannot begin to understand the true nature of emptiness.

We can infer from these lines of Maitripa's that the opposite is also true, if the root of faith is firm, the insight into non-duality will be firm. Faith here refers to faith in the three jewels; the Buddha, dharma and *sangha* – as they are presented in the Vajrayana. The Buddha is the Completely Awakened One who teaches the dharma. The dharma in this case refers to the tantras, particularly the Anuttarayoga tantra, which includes the father, mother and non-dual tantras. The sangha in this case is the lineage of Indian and Tibetan siddhas, who, have practiced the instructions and realized their meaning. The point is that without firm faith in the three jewels of the Vajrayana, the insight, which is the experience of the meaning of the Vajrayana, cannot be attained.

The second verse deals with the need for compassion:

2. If you do not develop unbiased compassion the two form kayas will not be attained.

The second point is that we should develop compassion. If we have not developed compassion at the time of the ultimate fruition of Buddhahood, there will be no spontaneous manifestation of the two form kayas (the *sambhogakaya* and the *nirmanakaya*) to benefit other beings.[19] So we should develop strong compassion without any partiality or bias.

The source of enlightened activity is compassion. The cause for Buddhahood is the two form bodies arising due to the compassion that has been generated by the Buddha during his training. In this case, the two form bodies are the supreme nirmanakaya and the sambhogakaya. The nirmanakaya helps beings with impure perception and the sambhogakaya helps beings with pure perception.

As ordinary practitioners we have impure perception and must engage in activity that is beneficial for others, rather than the extraordinary compassion that is totally without the bias of the division of "I" and "others." Compassion without bias is practiced by beings with pure perception and compassion based on the recognition that everyone, without distinction, wishes to be happy and to avoid suffering. Therefore everyone is equally fit to be a recipient of compassion.

The third verse contains the third instruction:

3. If the three prajnas are not practiced, realization will not arise.

The third instruction is that we should train in developing spiritual understanding (Skt. *prajna*).[20] If we don't have this spiritual understanding, we will not be able to gain realization of the true nature of phenomena, the most important point of the whole practice. We should try to develop spiritual understanding as much as possible. This is developed in three ways: through study, through contemplation, and through meditation.

To develop a genuine realization it is necessary to first develop stable meditation or *samadhi*. To do this we have to train in the three aspects of supreme knowledge called the three prajnas. Without doing this it is impossible to give birth to genuine realization. The term *prajna* literally means "*supreme* or *full* understanding." There are, of course, many different kinds of knowledge. For example, some are very knowledgeable in ways of harming others such as hunting, but this is not what is implied by the three prajnas. There are individuals who are very knowledgeable in mundane sciences such as geology, but this too is not prajna as it is meant here. What is meant here is a type of knowledge that is of endless benefit to ourselves and others, that is, the knowledge to help sentient beings achieve liberation. This is the prajna, or supreme knowledge, of the dharma.

The three prajnas are hearing, contemplating, and meditating. The first prajna of "hearing"[21] means being exposed to the words and instructions of the Buddha, of Buddhist scholars and of the siddhas. The second prajna of contemplation means actually thinking about what has been learned. Finally, the third prajna of meditation is the actual application in meditation of what has been understood through contemplation, and this internalization or absorption, samadhi, leads to realization.

The fourth verse reads:

4. If you do not attend the jetsun guru the two siddhis will not be attained.

The fourth instruction is that we should rely on our jetsun, or *root guru*. Without reliance on a guru, it is impossible to discover the true aspects of spiritual accomplishment. This means that in the short term we will not be able to achieve ordinary spiritual accomplishments and, in the long term, we will not be able to achieve final realization. The reason it is impossible to achieve realization without the help of a guru is that while practicing on the path, we have all sorts of experiences and impressions. Without someone to explain what is happening and how to react to the various things going on in the mind, we can easily go down an incorrect path. We can't expect to find spiritual guidance from books or from other ordinary persons. We need to have a guru who has enough realization and insight to guide us through these experiences so that we stay on the right path. With the help of a proper guru, we will be able to achieve all the aspects of spiritual accomplishment.

The two *siddhis* are the two results of correct practice, which are the supreme and the common siddhis. The supreme siddhi is full awakening, which is the abandonment of ignorance and the disturbing emotions.

In addition to the supreme siddhi of enlightenment there are lesser accomplishments, the common siddhis. These are extra-sensory perception, miraculous powers, and the ability to deal skillfully with a variety of situations. To attain either siddhi it is absolutely necessary to rely upon an authentic guru. We can attain the result of practice only if we rely on a qualified teacher and receive the appropriate instructions and put these instructions into practice. We cannot attain anything by simply practicing under our own power. Nor can we practice effectively based on information obtained from books. Even if the book is absolutely correct, it is still likely that we will misunderstand what the book says or develop doubt or confusion about its meaning.

The fifth verse says:

5. If you have not cut the root of mind, do not carelessly amend an awareness.

The fifth instruction is that we should guard our mind very carefully. When we begin meditation practice, we are overpowered by negativity and are caught going hither and thither by our anger, our jealousy, our desire and our ignorance. So we have to keep our mind in check. The best way to do this is to go straight to the root of the mind, which is the understanding of the nature of the mind. Once the nature of the mind is actually understood, then the other problems dissolve. So in the beginning we shouldn't allow ourselves to be pulled about by the various mental movements, but try to keep watch over our mind.

There are instructions in meditation where we are told to simply relax the mind and not engage in any effort whatsoever. However, this instruction can only be effective after we have already cut the root of mind. Cutting the root of mind means recognizing the mind's nature, that is, to cut through all doubts about the nature of the mind. So if we have totally experienced the mind's nature, we will have no fear and no doubt, and then relaxation of mind is possible. But until that point, if we simply relax, we will just wander further into the disturbing emotions and ignorance. So the point of these two lines is that until we have cut through the root of mind, it is necessary to engage in continual mindfulness and awareness.

The sixth verse is:

6. If you cannot strike phenomena with mudra, you should not retreat into great bliss.

The sixth instruction concerns experiences in meditation. In meditation there are many different experiences including pleasant feelings of wellbeing and bliss. The instruction is that when we are beginners, we shouldn't allow ourselves to be carried away by this great feeling of happiness. This is because at this stage we haven't realized emptiness yet, and therefore will not be able to integrate this experience of bliss into our practice. If we become attached to this feeling of bliss, then there is a great risk that it will become an obstacle to our practice.

This verse refers to the fact that, at some point, our mind must come to rest in an experience of bliss, which is the total pacification of all the disturbing emotions. For this to occur, all experience has to be sealed with the recognition of the emptiness of all experience. The term *mudra* here means "seal." "To strike phenomena with mudra," means to seal all phenomena with the recognition of its emptiness. The first six instructions emphasize what should be practiced. The next verses deal with what should be abandoned.

The seventh verse is:

7. If thoughts of desire arise you should act like a joyful elephant.

The instruction concerns attachment. In general, we should avoid having excessive attachment or involvement with outer objects or inner experiences of meditation. The way to deal with the feeling of attachment when it arises is not to stop the thought forcibly, nor to follow it. Rather we should remain immersed in non-conceptualization, that is, not creating any particular thoughts about it.

A good practitioner is not usually troubled by attachment or fixation, but sometimes through force of habit, thoughts of attachment or fixation arise. In this situation, Maitripa says, "Act as a joyful elephant." The term elephant signifying tremendous strength, and refers more specifically to the power of samadhi. So the joyful elephant means that we should engage in that very strong and unshakable samadhi that vanquishes thoughts.

This leads to the eighth verse, which is:

8. If occasionally the disturbing emotions arise look at the mind and meditate without distraction.

The instruction here is to not be overpowered by disturbing emotions. When any disturbing emotions arise, we shouldn't allow ourselves to be overpowered or carried away by them. Instead, we should remain in a state of meditation without distraction. The way to deal with these disturbing emotions is to look directly at their essence. If we can look straight at the essence of the negative emotions, they will automatically disappear. So we shouldn't be distracted or carried away by negativity.

When practitioners engage in the practice of extraordinarily profound dharma, they become capable of gradually decreasing the power of the disturbing emotions and gradually removing ignorance. But while that process is occurring, the disturbing emotions will still arise through force of habit, which has been accruing throughout beginningless time. Sometimes the practitioner will be able to cope with the disturbing emotions and sometimes not.

When the practitioner cannot abandon the disturbing emotions, one of two things can happen. He or she will either experience tremendous anxiety or fear about the presence of the disturbing emotion or he or she might simply dive in and follow the obscuration wherever it leads. Maitripa's advice is to not to follow or be seduced by the disturbing emotion or to fear it and treat it as an enemy. The remedy is to look at the nature of the mind that is experiencing the disturbing emotion and recognize that the disturbing emotion is simply an expression of the mind. We should look at the nature of the mind and try to determine the characteristics of that mind. By engaging in this type of examination, the disturbing emotion will be naturally pacified.

The ninth verse is:

9. If the mind is harmed by unfavorable conditions practice the four empowerments continually.

The ninth instruction concerns difficulties, troubles and physical problems in meditation. We might feel unwell, have a serious problem or experience extreme negativity. When this happens, we should either use our *yidam* practice or our *guru yoga* practice and take the four empowerments (Skt. *abhishekas*). The first empowerment, of body, is called the "vase empowerment." The second empowerment, of speech, is called the "secret empowerment." The third empowerment, of mind, is called the "jnana (wisdom-knowledge) empowerment." The fourth empowerment is called the "understanding of the true nature of phenomena (word)." Whenever we feel we are at a dead end and everything is very difficult, we should take these four empowerments. Then we will feel that our mind and the pure mind of the guru or yidam have completely and inseparably joined. Accomplishing this, we will find that these difficulties can be solved and that they gradually disappear.

Even when our practice is stable, situations may still arise that disturb it. We might even be very happy to the point of distraction. Or things may become very unpleasant and we may begin to suffer so much that we can't practice normally. When these impediments arise, this is the time to take the four empowerments. This consists of visualizing our root guru – or yidam deity – in front of us in space. We begin by visualizing rays of white light coming from his or her forehead and purifying the obscurations of our body, bestowing upon us the vase empowerment. Then from the guru's throat come rays of red light that strike and enter our own throat, purifying the obscurations of our speech and granting us the secret empowerment. Then from the guru's heart come rays of blue light that contact and enter our body at the center of the heart, granting us the wisdom empowerment. Then from the same three places come rays of light of the same three colors that strike and enter the same three places of our body all at once. At this time we should think that we have received the transmission or "*pointing-out*" *instruction* of the fourth empowerment, which purifies obscurations that affect body, speech and mind. We should think that, as a result of this empowerment, we have attained the realization of the true nature of reality (Skt. *dharmata*). This practice will cause the obstacles to our practice to be dispelled. This also means that they probably won't arise but that if they do, it won't be a big deal.

The tenth verse is:

10. *If disturbing emotions arise in your being remember the guru's instructions.*

The tenth instruction is that we shouldn't let ourselves be dominated by disturbing emotions whenever they crop up. We must remember that these disturbing emotions are marked by emptiness and we should not allow them to take over, but always keep them in check. If we find that a negative emotion is getting very strong, we should try to remember very clearly the instructions of our guru.

Whenever a disturbing emotion arises, if we can directly recognize its nature, then it is self-pacified without posing any problem. But even experienced practitioners will still find that sometimes no matter how hard they try, they can't seal a disturbing emotion that has arisen with *suchness*; the practitioner can't embrace it with emptiness and finds him or herself under the power of anger or attachment or ignorance. In this situation, the remedy is to bring to mind the actual instructions on the antidote for this particular disturbing emotion or to remember the general meditation instructions of the guru. The point is that as long as we can bring these instructions to mind, they will pacify the disturbing emotions. If we don't remember them, then we won't be able to pacify the disturbing emotions. This brings us to the eleventh verse:

11. If you do not supplicate one-pointedly, how can you fulfill the intentions of the holy ones?

The eleventh instruction is to pray to our guru with perfect concentration. It is necessary to pray to our guru and all the great masters to receive their *blessings*[22] so that we can integrate this blessing within our being. If we do not receive this blessing, then we will not be able to develop all their qualities and integrate these qualities within us. To develop all these qualities we must pray with full concentration to our guru and to the lamas of our lineage, praying that all their qualities can arise within us.[23]

Fulfilling the intentions of the holy ones means to actually generate in our mind the very same realization that the root and lineage gurus generated and have. To actually bring this about we must first generate a genuine faith and strong devotion in the root and lineage gurus. If we supplicate one-pointedly, then somehow their realization is transferred to us. Without devotion, this process of transference can't take place. The twelfth verse is:

12. If you do not meditate in the union of creation and completion, how can you realize the inseparability of samsara and nirvana?

The twelfth instruction relates to yidam meditation.[24] There are two stages of meditation: the creation stage (Skt. *utpattikrama*) and the completion stage (Skt. *sampannakrama*). But these two stages have to be practiced simultaneously. While doing visualization practice, we must at the same time do the completion stage practice. If not practiced simultaneously, we will not be able to realize the inseparability of present existence and liberation, that is, of *samsara* and *nirvana*. We will not be able to realize that within samsara there is the realization of the ultimate true nature of phenomena.

To realize the inseparability of samsara and nirvana, it is necessary to remove the foundation of the continual production of disturbing emotions. This root is the fixation and strong belief in the reality of ordinary appearances, which causes an impure outlook. To cut through the process of appearances, we must correctly identify our fixation and belief in the reality of ordinary appearances. We must realize how strong and persistent it is. Then, instead of identifying with the impure projections of our own mind and the world, we may instead conceive of ourselves in the form of a yidam. This process is the creation stage of yidam practice.

However, simply conceiving of ourselves in the form of a yidam is not sufficient because we might develop the idea that the yidam is an actual being with its own mind and personality. We might also begin to believe that the offerings and praises we make to it please the yidam. So it is important to cut through this misconception that the yidam has any inherent existence or that the yidam is some kind of god or goddess to be propitiated. Therefore, in the completion stage we recognize that the visualization is totally insubstantial.

The point is that in order to attain the realization of the inseparability of samsara and nirvana it is necessary for our meditation to include both the *sacred outlook* of the creation stage and the recognition of the insubstantiality of that sacredness.

Those were the twelve instructions of Maitripa to Marpa. However, there is one more verse:

13. This is a vajra song of twelve instructions, remembering these makes thirteen.

These are the twelve instructions given by Maitripa to which he added one more point: always keep the twelve points in mind. And then Maitripa said to Marpa, "If these thirteen points can be with you all the time, in the future you will definitely achieve the thirteenth *bodhisattva level* (which is Buddhahood).

The point of the last two lines is that the implementation of these twelve instructions depends completely upon remembering the instructions with uninterrupted mindfulness and awareness. So the thirteenth verse runs through the other twelve verses and therefore is not enumerated separately in the name of the song. In other words, mindfulness is the basis for all the other instructions.

The biography of Marpa goes on to say: "Thus Maitripa sang. Marpa was delighted with these instructions and assimilated them." When it says "delighted" it means that Marpa was intensely excited and pleased with these instructions, in the sense that he fully recognized their importance and usefulness. By hearing these instructions, he developed an uncommon faith in Maitripa and firmly resolved to put the instructions into practice, which he did.

If we look carefully at the biography of Marpa we will get some idea of how helpful these instructions were to Marpa. When Marpa was returning to Tibet at the completion of his first journey, all of the texts that he had accumulated over this twelve-year period of intense endeavor were thrown into the Ganges River by his jealous companion, Nyö Lotsawa, who had accompanied Marpa to India. As explained earlier, Marpa had a strong tendency towards anger and pride. Yet in this situation where he could easily have become enraged, he didn't react with any aggression whatsoever. He showed absolute patience and perhaps we can trace his development of patience to dharma instructions such as these.

4

Marpa Returns to Tibet

arpa left India to go back to Tibet, and he traveled with his companion Nyö Lotsawa. On the way difficulties arose from Nyö Lotsawa's feelings of jealousy towards Marpa's accomplishments in India. This led to the loss of the texts[25] that Marpa had collected. The problem of jealousy is typical of our human life in conditioned existence. There is no special quality attached to these incidents and these problems. They are only a manifestation of the difficulties that are inherent in the very nature of samsara.

On his way back to Tibet, Marpa was to have a dream in which he would meet Saraha, the great Indian mahasiddha and forefather of the Mahamudra lineage. Accounts of this dream are also found in Marpa's life story and in the *Rain of Wisdom*. In the dream, Saraha would give him a teaching to enable him to gain very deep insight and understanding. But first Marpa had to reach the border between Nepal and Tibet, where there was a little village called Lishokara. When he attempted to enter Tibet, customs officials detained him because at that time travelers had to pay a tax to cross the border. Marpa did not have any money so he stayed in Lishokara for a few days. The night before he was due to enter Tibet, he had the dream. In the dream dakinis appeared to him and said, "You must go to Shri Parvata Mountain in the south." Marpa replied that he didn't know how to get there and the dakinis said, "Don't worry about it, we will take you." In the dream they escorted him to the mountain where he met the great siddha Saraha. When he actually saw Saraha, the dream became more real than any ordinary dream. He was technically asleep and dreaming, but in his dream he received definite instructions from Saraha that he had not received from anyone previously. Marpa didn't encounter Saraha physically, he encountered Saraha's wisdom body.

As a result of the dream, he found that he had gained new insight into understanding the Mahamudra. He then proceeded into Tibet and just beyond the border he was invited to stay with one of his disciples, the same disciple he had stayed with at the beginning of his journey to India.

While staying there, the disciple asked him, "You have been to India and studied a lot and have probably gained great realization. So I would be very grateful if you could give us a teaching of something that is new, something that you have never taught before." Marpa said that on his way from Nepal, customs officers had held him up at the border and that he had to stay in the Lishokara for a few days. He explained that while he was there, he had a dream in which he received instructions from Saraha. He said, "Now I'm going to sing this song of instructions from Saraha to you, so please listen attentively."

Marpa taught them the instructions in the form of a-story-and-a-song. He told them about what had happened, and in the middle of this, he sang parts of the instruction that he had received. He began:

Today is very auspicious and special. It is the tenth day of the lunar month and we have all gathered together for this great feast and this wonderful celebration of being together. You are people with great faith and all of you kept your commitments to your lama completely. Today you've asked me to give you a special teaching that you've never heard before. But I must admit that after having traveled to India, my body has gone through so much hardship that I'm very tired and don't think I will be able to sing a very good song. I'm not a good singer anyway and I'm not very clever with words; so I don't think I can do this very well. But since all of you, my friends, are kindly requesting, I don't want to ignore your kindness to me and I will try to sing something to you. Since you asked me for something new, I will tell you in my song what happened when I met the great mahasiddha Saraha in my dream. Now please hearken to my song and try to keep it in mind.

I was held up by customs at the border because these people are very strict and they didn't know that I own absolutely nothing. They are very, very adamant. And for a humble traveler like me, it was difficult and that is why I had to stay there for a few days. But during one of the last days I was there, I had a dream. In my dream I saw two very beautiful Indian maidens and they told me, "You ought to go to Shri Parvata, the southern Mountain of Splendor." I replied that I had never been to this place nor had I ever seen or heard of it. "I have no experience traveling there and I do not know the way."

But the two girls replied, "We are like your sisters, so don't worry. We will take you there without any trouble."

They then took a piece of cloth and formed it into a kind of hammock. When Marpa sat on this hammock, they carried him through space and in an instant he arrived at the Mountain of Splendor. There he saw a magnificent tree and in the shade of the tree sat Saraha. Marpa had never seen anyone so incredibly majestic, sitting with two consorts by his side and wearing bone ornaments. He looked incredibly joyful and was smiling at Marpa saying, "Hello my son. Have you had a nice journey? How was it on the way?" Immediately, Marpa felt tremendous joy and had tears streaming from his eyes because he was so moved. His entire flesh dripped with an incredible effluence of faith and the hairs of his body stood on end. With this amazing feeling of fervor and devotion, he prostrated to Saraha and placed Saraha's feet on top of his head.[26] Then Marpa said, "Father, please look upon me with your great compassion." At this moment Marpa received all the great blessings of body, speech, and mind.

Saraha placed his hand on top of Marpa's head giving him the blessing of the body. Immediately this created in Marpa a tremendous feeling of bliss and well being, which is called the experience of "untainted bliss." This bliss is compared to the experience of incredible happiness that one can have when one is high or drunk, like an elephant that's drunk too much. Marpa had received the blessing of speech in the form of Saraha's initial greeting. These few words had such an impact on him that they brought about the blessing of mind, which created a completely new, fresh insight in Marpa's awareness. The new insight that Marpa gained was totally inexpressible. It was similar to the experience of a dumb person who has a dream but can never tell anyone of the experience because he cannot talk. As a result of this blessing of mind, Marpa realized the meaning of *dharmakaya* and emptiness just as they are. He said that his experience was like being a corpse, meaning that a corpse doesn't have any thoughts or sensations. So in this vision Marpa realized the entire world just as it was, without any conceptualization on his part.

Marpa continued his story, "Then Saraha sang his spiritual song of advice. He sang it with the most beautiful melody and in a very smooth and gentle voice:

Namo (which means, "I pay homage" or "I prostrate.") Emptiness and compassion are inseparable and are unceasing. The continuity of these two is never broken. This is because from the very beginning, they are within the mind. They have not been created anew. They are part of the very nature, the natural condition of the mind. They are continually there.

Where does one find the root of this? It is found in the mind. And that is why one should guard one's mental consciousness very carefully. When one looks for the essence of the mind, look at the present instant. Don't become involved with the moment before or the moment that will come later. The whole point of meditation is to be within the nature of the mind.

If one interferes and changes things, that is not meditation. The point of meditation is to let the mind be within the true nature of the mind. It isn't a matter of thinking it is like this or like that. The true way to meditate is to leave the mind in an unaltered state, without changing or interfering with anything. This has to be initiated at the very instant the mind is there.

If one can let the mind be unaltered, then one will gain liberation from samsara. When one lets the mind be within its own nature, it should be as a child who looks at things in a wide-eyed, completely natural way. If one can do this, one will feel as fearless as a lion. One must let the mind rest within itself just as a wild elephant roams about just as it likes. Just let the mind be completely relaxed and free. It is like a bee going from flower to flower. Let the mind be completely relaxed, free, and natural within its own nature. When one meditates, one mustn't look at samsara as being bad, filled with all sorts of faults. This is because the very nature of samsara will lead one to the true, essential nature of phenomena, the true nature of the mind. Also there is no need to think in terms of achieving Buddhahood because the very nature of the mind is the nature of the Buddha.

What is called the "ordinary mind"[27] is the mind as it is in itself, neither adulterated nor modified in any way. Normally, our mind is under the influence of thoughts and negativity and isn't in its ordinary condition. When one thinks, "I must meditate" this isn't the ordinary mind either. This is the mind that is modified, that is adulterated, that is changed. So let the mind be within itself and let it be within its own essence, which is naturally peaceful, relaxed, clear, and empty. One just has to rest within its nature without interfering, without changing anything, and let the mind be as it is in its freshness and immediacy without bringing about any change. If one will do this, then one can understand the true nature of mind, the true nature of everything. This points to the very essence of everything and is the very key of Mahamudra.

Marpa then said, "This is what I heard from Saraha.." He said that when he heard the entire spiritual song of Saraha, he woke up. When he awoke, all the words that Saraha had spoken were still very clear in his mind. He hadn't forgotten a single word. He also had a very vivid experience that was like the experience of coming out of darkness. All of a sudden it was as though all the very vivid intelligence of the mind had opened up and that the very nature of mind was lying open in front of him.

Now Marpa could see this incredible clarity of mind. It was like the sun when there are no clouds. As a result of this experience Marpa gained a decisive understanding and conviction of the validity of what he had been taught. He felt that even if all the Buddhas of the past, present and future were to appear before him, he wouldn't have anything to ask. This is because he was convinced that he completely understood the nature of the mind and the nature of phenomena, and there was nothing else to know. As a result he gained very decisive confidence in what he understood. Marpa continued:

Whatever advice one receives from a yidam or dakini or one's guru is very precious. It is something one must keep present in one's mind and that one must practice. It isn't something one should boast about or talk about with others because there is no point of going around and telling others about all the various signs and experiences that one has. One must keep whatever happens in one's mind like a precious jewel. But tonight there was a purpose in telling you about this because it is so meaningful. I never have mentioned this experience before tonight and you will see later whether I mention it again; tonight I had a particular purpose for sharing this experience with you.

This story is particularly meaningful because when I came from Tibet to go to India, I was all on my own. I had no support, no friends and lots of troubles. During this time all of you, my disciples, helped me and were very kind to me. I have never forgotten your kindness, so tonight out of gratitude I shared this very deep teaching with you. I pray that all the lamas and yidams and protectors may not be irritated by my sharing this profound teaching with you and that they may not look upon this as a fault of mine.

Following this story, Marpa was able to return to his native home of Lhotrak.

It is important to have some understanding of exactly who Saraha is in the context of the Mahamudra lineage. The extraordinary lineage of Mahamudra has both a short and a long lineage.[28] The short lineage is the passing of the Mahamudra teachings from Vajradhara directly to Tilopa and then from Tilopa on to Naropa to Marpa to Milarepa to Gampopa and so on to the present day. The long lineage is the transmitting of the Mahamudra teachings from Vajradhara to the bodhisattva Ratnamati, who transmitted them to Saraha, who transmitted them to Nagarjuna, to Shavari, to Maitripa who then transmitted them on to Marpa. So Saraha is extremely important for the Mahamudra lineage. Of course, it was impossible for Marpa to have met Saraha physically because Saraha had lived much earlier (in the 9th century C.E.). This encounter was not a dream that we might have, but Marpa was able to come face-to-face with the timeless wisdom body of Saraha.

5

Marpa Establishes the Teachings in Tibet

arpa had many great disciples and history records four famous ones, who were called "the four great pillars of the teaching." When Marpa returned from India and crossed the border from Nepal into Tibet he gave advice to his disciples with a spiritual song. The disciple at whose home he stayed was actually the very first disciple of the four great pillars. This disciple was named Ngoktön Chödor. The word "chödor" was the name of the place where he was from, which was Shung, Tibet. His actual name was Lotsa Choche.

When Marpa returned to Tibet he traveled to many places teaching the dharma, and acquired many other disciples who practiced the dharma under his guidance and progressed gradually along the various stages leading to enlightenment.

One day he was traveling with his servant and they met two yogis: a teacher and his disciple. The yogis approached Marpa and the yogi's disciple asked, "Where do you come from?" and "Where are you going?" Marpa's servant answered, "This is Marpa who went to India and became one of the greatest disciples of the great mahasiddha Naropa. Now he is traveling in Tibet to give the Vajrayana instructions to those who are spiritually mature enough to receive the teachings. By practicing his instructions, a person can achieve the ultimate fruition of the path. But even those who are not spiritually ready to practice these teachings will derive benefit just by hearing his words and meeting him. They will get a chance to establish a connection with Marpa and this will sow the seed of liberation and omniscience, the seed of Buddhahood, in their mind. This is why we have come here. Soon Marpa will have to return to India to obtain more teachings. To express his gratitude to his teachers, he must take some gold with him to India. He is now touring different places and giving teachings in order to collect offerings of gold to give to his teachers in India."

After meeting these two yogis Marpa met the disciple named Meton Sonam Gyaltsen, whom Marpa was to rename "Meton Tsonpo" and who was to become the second of Marpa's greatest disciples, one of the "four great pillars." Marpa gave him the empowerment of Hevajra and remained there in the Tsang Rang district of Tibet, teaching for two months.

Next, Marpa went north. In the same area, a trader named Marpa Golek, was passing through and saw a great gathering of people and asked what was going on there. Someone said, "There is a lama named Marpa who is a disciple of the famous mahasiddha Naropa and he is giving teachings and empowerments." When the trader heard this, he was surprised, thinking, "Oh, that's very strange. My name is also Marpa so maybe we come from the same family. He seems to be a good teacher, so maybe I should go and listen to him." He then went to meet Marpa and received teachings from him.

Afterwards, Marpa Golek offered Marpa Lotsawa some very nice clothes because he noticed that Marpa wasn't wearing anything new. He invited Marpa to visit him at his home. When Marpa arrived, he was still wearing the same old, ragged clothes. Marpa Golek was a bit surprised and thought, "Well, that's a little strange. I gave him these brand new clothes and he is still wearing the same old rags. What's going on? Maybe he is very attached to beautiful things and riches and can't even bear to wear them. Maybe this lama isn't as good as he's supposed to be." He then asked, "How come you're still wearing those old clothes. I offered you some nice new ones, and I know that some other people also gave you new clothes. Why do you keep wearing the same old ones?" Marpa replied, "Well, you see it's because I'm trying to go back to India to receive some more teachings and I need gold to go there and won't be able to get gold for old rags. So I keep on wearing the same clothes so that I can exchange all the new clothes for gold and go to India to obtain more teachings. That's why I keep on wearing the same old clothes." When Marpa Golek heard this, he was extremely impressed and realized that Marpa hadn't worn the new clothes because he wasn't involved in material things. This reinforced his faith in Marpa even more.

Marpa left the northern part of Tibet to return south towards his home in Lhotrak. There he was invited to teach by Dorje Tsultrim Wangnge who was to become his third greatest disciple of the "four great pillars" of teaching. Afterward, Marpa visited another place in the south where he met an important disciple named Baram Bawachen. The name "Bawachen" is actually a nickname that means "having a goiter."

Marpa had now made the connection to several of his main disciples. Ngoktön Chödor and Meton Tsonpo were given the Hevajra teachings. Dorje Tsultrim Wangnge and Marpa Golek were given the Guhyasamaja empowerments and teachings, and also the five levels of instructions on the completion stage of the "father tantra." Baram Bawachen received the Mahamaya teachings. In this way Marpa created the conditions for the spreading of the teachings in Tibet.[29]

Marpa's Second Trip to India

Following this period of putting in place many of his main disciples, Marpa prepared for his second journey to India.

By this time Marpa had started a family in Tibet, having married and had children. But in spite of this, he felt that it was still necessary to go back to India and continue what he had begun with his first journey.

Aside from relinquishing his attachment to his family, Marpa also had to meet the tremendous expense of another journey. Before going to India the first time, Marpa had received his inheritance from his parents and converted it into eighteen *srang* (in Tibetan, or *thal* in Indian) of gold. He converted everything into gold so that on the difficult and dangerous trails and roads to India he need only carry a small sack.

For his second trip to India Marpa took fifty *thals* of gold, which he had acquired with a great deal of exertion. Then when he went for the third time, he took a large bowl of gold dust and used it in offering for the teachings and texts that he brought back to Tibet and translated for the benefit of all Buddhist practitioners.

On Marpa's first journey, his traveling companion dumped all of Marpa's books of teachings and instructions into the water, which meant that when he returned to Tibet after the first journey, the only texts he had were those he had memorized. He had no written teachings with him at all: no *sadhana* texts, no liturgies, no commentaries, nothing. So everything he taught after this first journey came from his extensive memorization. He felt that he absolutely had to go back to India a second time to acquire copies of these texts for posterity and to receive additional instructions on them.

When Marpa was about to leave on his second journey, many of his disciples offered to accompany him as his servant. But Marpa wouldn't agree to this and went on his own. Once again he traveled through Nepal and met two lamas there. Then he proceeded to India where he went again to meet his teacher, Naropa.

From Naropa he received the three levels of empowerment of Hevajra. The first level is called the "very detailed empowerment;" the second level is "the middle length empowerment;" and the third level the "short empowerment." Marpa also received three tantras. He received the root tantra of Hevajra, called the "Hevajra-mula tantra" that he had already received during his first journey. Then he received two other tantras that provided more detailed explanations of this practice. These last two are more like tantras with an oral commentary, but they still came from the Buddha himself. One of these, called the "Dakini-varapanjara tantra" is a special tantra that provides an explanation of the Hevajra tantra. Marpa then received the tantra, called the "Sumputa tantra" that provides a general explanation of the others. These explanations and commentaries weren't just explanations of their terminology, but provided profound and in depth instruction for the practice of the root Hevajra tantras.

Naropa then advised Marpa to visit other teachers, because he said, "The last time when you came here, you received teachings from other masters, and now you should go and see them to clarify doubts and ask questions about what you've already learned. You should also receive from them whatever other teachings you didn't receive before."

Marpa first went to visit the great master Maitripa. From him he received all the teachings he had learned before and he made sure everything was very clear. He also received new teachings from Maitripa including the Guhyasamaja empowerment and the commentary on this tantra. He also received the tantras on Mahamudra that were taught by the Buddha and translated these into Tibetan. These are known as the *Mahamudra Tilaka*. Marpa then returned to Naropa for a while. Then he went to see his other teachers, Kukkuripa and Yeshe Nyingpo, with whom he reviewed the meaning of everything he had learned from them before.

After returning, Marpa stayed with Naropa for some time and received the Chakrasamvara teachings again. But this time Marpa received a different line of transmission of these teachings than the first one called the "Tradition of the King" that came from the Buddha through King Indrabhuti.

Following this transmission, Marpa made preparations to go back to Tibet again. Before Marpa was about to go, Naropa sang a very strange spiritual song of farewell with a very obscure meaning:

There is a man who is a flower in the sky and there is a son of a barren woman riding a horse who has a whip made of the hairs of a tortoise. She has a dagger that is made of a rabbit's horn and she kills the enemy within the true nature. At the moment of this killing, the dumb can speak, the blind can see, the deaf can hear, the lame can run and jump and the sun and moon are dancing.

When Naropa had finished singing this unusual song, he said, "You have to come back to India once more because I have many other instructions for you. If you do not return, you will never know the meaning of this song." Marpa didn't get a chance to further inquire about the song and just kept it all in his mind. Naropa said, "Just don't forget." So Marpa returned to Tibet remembering all of this, but not understanding a word of it.

When Marpa arrived in Tibet, he went to Tsang Rang where he saw Meton Sonam Gyaltsen. Meton's disposition in teaching and practice was luminosity and so Marpa gave Meton the Chakrasamvara empowerment and instructions, after which his name was changed to Meton Tsönpo. Following this, Marpa went back to his home of Lhotrak where he met his most famous disciple, the "fourth pillar," Milarepa. Marpa put Milarepa to the task of building a large stone mansion of nine stories for his eldest son, Darmadode. Milarepa went through many difficulties and hardships because Marpa asked him twice to dismantle it. These tasks were necessary for Milarepa's spiritual development.[30]

After Milarepa had gone through the tremendous difficulties of rebuilding again and again the high tower, Marpa treated him as a true disciple and sent him to practice in a little cave near his own home. While Milarepa was in the cave in Taknya, near Lhotrak, Marpa had a dream one night in which he saw three very beautiful dakinis singing a song in which they explained in great detail the meaning of the spiritual song that Naropa had sung to him before he left India. They sang:

The man who is a flower in the sky represents all the *jnana* (awareness) dakinis. The instructions that come from these dakinis are called the "whispered lineage of instruction of the dakinis," which concerns the emptiness of all phenomena and is represented by the son of the barren woman riding the horse. The great qualities that arise in one's mind after practicing the instructions are gained not through words, but through the actual understanding of practice. This is symbolized by the whip made with tortoise hair. The dagger with which the enemy was killed represents the unborn nature of all phenomena. The killing of the enemy within the true essence was done by Tilopa. Tilopa symbolizes the dumb person because when he realized the very essential nature of phenomena, he couldn't pass this instruction on through words. The blind man who began seeing was Naropa because Naropa was blind and then through Tilopa's instruction was able to see the truth of phenomena. The lame man who started running and jumping represents Marpa because he was unable to move within the realm of the essential truth of phenomena, but through the deep instructions he became able to do just that. Finally the sun and moon dancing refers to the yidams, Hevajra, Chakrasamvara, and Mahamaya.

So this explanation provided by the three dakinis who appeared in a dream to Marpa gave him the symbolic meaning of everything in Naropa's strange spiritual song. When Marpa woke up, he suddenly felt that the dream was a sign that he should go back to India very soon.

Meanwhile, Milarepa was still in retreat, practicing nearby. One night Milarepa had a dream in which he saw a girl with a bluish body wearing bone ornaments and very fine golden hairs above her lip. She said to him, "There is a very, very important instruction that makes it possible to achieve Buddhahood without terrible hardships. This is the instruction on the transference of consciousness and resuscitation of a corpse and is called the *phowa* instruction. You should definitely obtain this instruction by asking your guru to give it to you."

So Milarepa asked Marpa for this instruction and since this was a practice Marpa had not yet received from Naropa, Marpa took this as another sign that he should return to India very soon.

Following these two dreams Marpa made provisions to go to India. As told in the *Rain of Wisdom*,³¹ all of Marpa's disciples tried to dissuade him from going. They said, "You are no longer a young man. It's very difficult for an elderly person to travel all that distance. You've told us time and time again how difficult the journey is and it will be very dangerous if you try to go there now on your own. If anything happens to you, then all the instructions will be lost for us. Please don't go. Stay here. We are already very satisfied with the instructions we have here in Tibet. We don't need anything more. Please stay here and send your son Darmadode instead."

So they pleaded and pleaded with him, but Marpa said, "No. I have to go and I must go myself. If I were to send my son Darmadode who is very young and inexperienced with traveling, it would just cause me much worry about his safety and whether he would be able to find the correct instructions. So I must go myself. Anyway when I left Naropa, I told him that I would return, not that I would send him my son. We have a saying that even if a trader is very old, he is also very experienced. He knows the way well and so he won't get into trouble. I know the way and even if I die, I'm going to go." Then Marpa sang a spiritual song:

I pay homage to Naropa and Maitripa. Now I'm going to revisit my master Naropa. I promised to go and it is very important for me to go there now. The dakinis have pointed the way for me. Also when I think of my guru, I can't help but go. There is no way for me not to go. The way is difficult indeed.

First there is a very wide, long plain of plains. It's very, very broad and even horses get tired traversing it. But I have no fear of traveling there because I have a special instruction that will enable me to ride the horse of prana with my mind. So I can travel through this plain very easily.

On my way to India, there will be the high passes that are very cold and sometimes frozen. But I do not fear them because I have the instructions of tummo, which provides me with a great blazing fire. No clothes of any kind could ever compare with this. So I know there will be no trouble on my way to India.

In Nepal there is great heat and I am not afraid of this because I have instructions to experience everything as being of one taste. I feel everything exactly the same whether it is hot or cold. This is better than any ordinary remedy, so I'm not afraid. There will be no trouble on my way to India.

The great Ganges River is very wide and frightening, but I have no fear because I have the instructions that make it possible for me to fly, with my mind I can ride over anything. No boats of any kind could match this. So I'm going to India and there will be no trouble crossing the Ganges.

Although there is much famine in the savage lands of India, I'm not worried because I have an instruction that enables me to live on just a few drops of water. No ordinary food or drink could ever compare with this. So I will travel to India and there will be no trouble.

On the way there are robbers and thieves in the wild and remote places. But I have the instructions that enable me to render robbers harmless. No ordinary human strength can be matched by this power. So I will go to India and there will be no trouble.

Why do I go to India? I'm going to India because my great teachers Naropa and Maitripa are in India. Kukkuripa is also in India. And the very precious Mahabodhi statue[32] is also in India. So whatever happens, no matter what fate I meet. Even if it costs me my life, I am going to India.

6

Marpa's Third Visit to India

arpa's third visit to India was fraught with difficulties. He had to go through tremendous hardships and troubles and only because he was so full of confidence and devotion to his lama was he able to endure this trip. As a result of his wish to practice the dharma, his diligence in practice became even greater, making it possible to achieve the ultimate realization.

When Marpa arrived at the border of Nepal and India, he met the great teacher Atisha. He felt great faith in Atisha who was a very good monk and a very great pandita. Atisha was one of Marpa's thirteen teachers in India. He received an empowerment from Atisha and afterwards they spoke together. Marpa asked where Naropa was and Atisha replied, "He has started to live like a yogi." At some point in their lives greatly accomplished beings start to behave in a way that is completely beyond the grasp of ordinary people.[33] Everything they do is within the realm of miracles and the extraordinary, and their behavior becomes totally unpredictable. One can't even tell where they are and where to meet them. They might be living at the top of the mountain or on a beach or on the bank of a lake. But at this point it is sometimes possible for disciples with great faith to meet their teacher. But sometimes they still cannot meet them even with great faith. Atisha explained that Naropa had taken up this kind of life and that presently he was mostly likely teaching non-human disciples (such as dakinis and *dakas*). Therefore, Atisha added, "It would be very difficult for you to meet him and, in fact, Naropa doesn't even know that you are coming. So maybe you might be better off staying with me for some time and working on translations and then going back to Tibet. Maybe that would be a better and more beneficial course of action."

Marpa was saddened by this news but said, "Well, no matter whether I actually get to meet him or not, I have to go because I promised that I would return the last time I met Naropa. I really must go and try to meet him." He felt a very strong conviction, an intuitive feeling that he would get to meet Naropa even though Naropa had now taken up the lifestyle of a yogi. So he carried on with his journey and reached Nepal.

In Nepal he met two lamas, Lama Sechen and Lama Pundrakpa, from his previous journeys and he asked them where Naropa could be found. They gave the same answer as Atisha, saying, "These days it seems that Naropa is living the life of a mahasiddha, so it will be very difficult to meet him. You might not get to see him at all." As soon as Marpa heard this, his heart sank and he felt utterly depressed. But at the same time he felt that he ought to try and ask the two lamas, "Do you think that means I won't get a chance to meet him again?" The two lamas replied, "Well, there is something in your favor because you are the kind of disciple who has always kept his dharma commitments perfectly, so your link with your lama is perfectly intact. Also your lama, Naropa, has the wisdom that is all seeing, the highest kind of spiritual perception. So when there is the connection of a disciple who has kept all of his dharma commitments and a lama who has spiritual vision, it is possible that you will meet him if you really make prayers and offerings."

So Marpa continued on and arrived in India. He went straight to Naropa's dwelling and found Naropa's servant, Prajnasimha. Marpa spoke with him, but the servant said, "What a shame. You arrived too late. Naropa left last year on the fifteenth day of the first month." Then Marpa said, "Well, I've come because I've been given the order to try to find the teachings of the *whispered transmission* of the dakinis.

54

Do you know if this teaching is still taught here in India?" The servant replied that he had heard of many different kinds of instructions, but had never heard of this particular teaching. But he added, "When Naropa left, he said that you would come and asked me to give you his *vajra*, bell and *thangka* of your yidam, Hevajra. But unfortunately, the vajra and bell have been stolen but I have kept the thangka very carefully and here it is." He gave Marpa the thangka and Marpa felt such an amazing outburst of faith and devotion towards Naropa that he broke into tears. Then the servant told him not to forget that Naropa had the eyes of wisdom and could see him and hear his prayers. Then he said, "I feel quite sure that if you pray to him, you will meet him." Marpa then went to see Maitripa who said more or less the same thing: if Marpa prayed to Naropa, he might get to meet him.

Then Marpa went to visit some other masters from whom he had received teachings previously. He went to see Kukkuripa and several others and received instructions from them. He also asked each of them if they could give him a special method to find Naropa. All of them said the same thing, that if he prayed to Naropa and felt enough genuine faith and devotion, he would get to meet him.

Marpa continued his search for eight months. Sometimes he was completely on his own and sometimes Lama Sechen or Lama Pundrakpa accompanied him. He would go from forest to forest, from mountain to mountain, on and on and on. But he never found Naropa. Sometimes he would suddenly have the impression that he had seen Naropa or had heard some of Naropa's words coming from space. Or he would have dreams of Naropa, but he never actually met him. It was just an impression that he would get from time to time.

After eight months of searching, Marpa came to the point where he was very desperate. One day while sitting very depressed reading a text, he got this very, very strong feeling that he was going to meet Naropa. He jumped up to his feet and ran to a forest nearby looking here and there for Naropa. All of a sudden he came upon a shepherd and gave the shepherd a big piece of gold and said, "Please tell me if you've seen or heard anyone called Naropa." And the shepherd replied, "Well, I think he must have gone through here because these could be his footprints" pointing down to two footprints in the rock.

As soon as Marpa saw the footprints of Naropa, he felt tremendously happy and his devotion to his teacher grew greater and greater. With longing, he looked up into the sky and saw a beautiful sandalwood tree in front of him. In the sandalwood tree, he saw the complete *mandala* of Hevajra. It was very small, but all the details were completely there. There was Hevajra and the nine deities that make up this mandala each with its specific color and specific attributes. Immediately Marpa knew that this must be an emanation of Naropa. So he prostrated to this mandala and made prayers and offerings. Then he saw Hevajra's consort, Nairatmya in the mandala. In her heart was the mantra of Hevajra in a very small circle. The mantra wheel was actually a wheel of eight syllables; it was there, very, very tiny, but very clear and complete. It was as though it had been drawn with the tip of a hair because it was so fine. And from the mantra radiated lights of all colors, which penetrated Marpa's heart. When this light came into him, he felt that he had received all the blessings of the body, speech and mind of Hevajra. This, of course, filled him with very great joy and happiness and reinforced his longing for his guru. He kept on praying and praying to Naropa and in a flash, Naropa appeared in front of him in the dress of a mahasiddha with all the bone ornaments saying, "Here I am. I've come to you."

Marpa was so happy when he saw Naropa that he fainted. When he came to, he immediately made a mandala offering with all the gold that he had carried from Tibet. But Naropa said, "I'm not interested in gold and don't need gold." And Marpa replied, "I know a lama doesn't need gold, but I need to complete the accumulation of virtue. Also all my friends and disciples in Tibet who contributed to this offering have to complete their accumulation of virtue. So please, for our sake, accept this offering."

Naropa then took the offering and said, "Now I offer all of this to my guru and the three jewels." Saying this he took the gold and threw it all over the forest. At this point, Marpa felt, on one hand, very happy that his guru had accepted the offering and, on the other hand, thought that it was a waste; he had gone through so much hardship to get all this gold together. He also thought of all the difficulties his disciples had gone through to help collect the gold.

Then Naropa joined his hands at the level of his heart as in a gesture of prayer. He opened his hands and said, "Don't worry, the gold is not wasted. I don't need it. But if somebody wants it, it's here" and all the gold was again in his hands. Then once again, Naropa said, "I do not need gold, but if anyone wants it, here is some gold." He stamped his foot and everything around him turned into gold.

After he had done this, Naropa said, "It seems that you've been brought to me through the great kindness of Tilopa." He then quoted a prediction that had been made by Tilopa concerning Marpa: "At the monastery of Phullahari the great son of pure intelligence would dispel the darkness of ignorance in the mind of the intelligent one, Marpa, Chokyi Lodro. It would dispel the darkness in the mind of the intelligent one and then the great brilliance of jnana would shine."

Then Naropa added, "This means that we have to go together to Phullahari (which in Tibetan is "the flower with a very beautiful, colorful radiance") and I will transmit all the instructions to you." So both of them, spiritual father and son, left together for Phullahari.

At Phullahari, Marpa requested instruction from Naropa. He asked for the whispered transmission of the dakinis and the phowa practice for the transference of consciousness and resuscitation of a dead corpse with one's consciousness. When Marpa made these requests, Naropa asked him if this idea was his own or whether he had been told by the dakinis to request the first teaching. Marpa replied, "No, this is not my own idea nor did the dakinis tell me to get these teachings. It was my disciple, Thöpaga (Milarepa) who was told by the dakinis to receive these teachings." Then Naropa explained, "How amazing! Tibet is this dark, northern land where the Buddha's teaching were not known. But now there is a person who is like the sun rising in that dark country. I bow down in homage to this person named Thöpaga (Milarepa)." Thus Naropa bent his head three times in the direction of the north and while he was bending his head, all the landscape such as the mountains and trees took the same shape and bent towards the north where Tibet was.

While Marpa was with Naropa at Phullahari, he also received the complete empowerments and instructions for the several kinds of Chakrasamvara practices: the mandala with sixty-two deities, the mandala of thirteen deities, the mandala with five deities and the mandala of Chakrasamvara alone with his consort. For the Chakrasamvara mandala, the empowerment was given with the help of a mandala drawn on the crown with various colors depicted in colored sands. Marpa also received the whole cycle of mandalas for Vajrayogini practice: the one with fifteen deities, the one with seven deities, the one with five deities, and the one with Vajrayogini alone as the deity. The picture of the mandala of Vajrayogini was made with yellow powder. With these instructions on the mandalas, Marpa had received the complete instructions of Naropa.

Following this, Naropa informed Marpa that everything he had been taught up to this point was like the outer skin of a person, but that what he had just been given was the very essence of all the teachings. Naropa instructed him that "This should be kept as a single line of transmission, being transmitted only from one teacher to one disciple, and so on. It should be kept like this for thirteen generations, and if this is done, the teaching will later spread and develop in a very strong and very beneficial way."

Marpa was completely convinced that what he had been given was really a very special method of practice. As far as his understanding was concerned, it was the same now as it had been before. The nature of the realization was unchanged. The great difference was that these methods made it possible to obtain realization very quickly. Naropa continued, saying:

In my days, I went through many difficulties. I had to endure twelve great hardships and twenty-four very difficult tasks. This was done by my guru, Tilopa, to test my faith and devotion. You also had to go through a lot of difficulties. You've come to India three times at the risk of your life and you have also had to endure many difficulties and face a lot of fears. But Tilopa had told me that you were the kind of disciple who would be capable of putting up with such hardships. That is why I put you through these difficulties and I now appoint you as my representative.

Then Naropa said to Marpa, "Now look up into the sky. There is the complete mandala of Hevajra in nine aspects." When Marpa looked up, he saw the whole incredibly clear and vivid mandala of Hevajra in its nine aspects in the sky above him

Naropa then said, "Now your yidam has come. Where will you prostrate first? Are you going to prostrate to the yidam first or to me first?"

Marpa was so overwhelmed with the vividness of the presence of the yidam that he prostrated to the yidam first.

Naropa simply commented, "If there is no guru, then there won't be any Buddha. All the thousand Buddhas of this eon depend on their guru to become Buddhas. The yidam is only the emanation of the guru. You should know this and you have made a minor mistake this time. This means that your family line will not be very long."

Although Marpa had seven sons, it meant that his family line wouldn't carry on. But Naropa added that since Marpa had prostrated to his yidam, this meant that his dharma line would be very great and that it would continue for as long as the Buddha's teachings would remain on this earth. So he said, "Rejoice, because your dharma line will be very great, very strong and very long."

However, Marpa felt upset and depressed because he thought, "I've been studying all these years. I know very well that the yidam is much less important than the guru. When I meditate, I always visualize myself as the yidam with the guru being on top of my head. I know very well that the guru is the most important one. I also experienced this very strongly when I saw the mandala of the yidam in the sandalwood tree. This wasn't half as meaningful to me as meeting with my guru later on. Why have I made such a mistake today? There must be something wrong with me."

Then, while Marpa was with Naropa, he became physically quite ill. All of his dharma friends and the other disciples of Naropa said, "We should ask the guru to do a spiritual practice to help your health." But Marpa replied, "Well, that wouldn't be suitable because now I've given the guru everything I had and I don't have any more offerings to present to him to make prayers for me. But I feel that if this is the right time for dharma to develop in Tibet, I'm not going to die here. If the protectors of the dharma are truly protecting the teachings, then they won't allow me to die here in India. Also there is nothing better for healing me than praying to my guru and the three jewels." With this attitude Marpa got better and overcame his illness.

Marpa's sadness, however, remained. To dispel it, Naropa put on a large offering feast and during this feast, Naropa gave some very profound instructions on the Six Yogas of Naropa to show just how incredibly fortunate Marpa was:

> You are very fortunate because you have a very precious human birth. But even more fortunate is that you have the instructions on subtle heat (Tib. *tummo*) practice through which you can meditate on a deity as being just a creation, a conjuration. You can meditate on the three *nadis* and the four *chakras*. Through these meditations you can gain the experience of bliss, clarity, and emptiness. Did you benefit from these tummo instructions?
>
> You also have the second instruction on the *illusory body* through which you can meditate outwardly on the

emptiness of all phenomena. Inwardly, you can have experiences that are completely ineffable, that cannot be expressed in words. Have you found these instructions on the illusory body to be of help?

You have the third instruction on the *dream practice*. Through this practice when you meditate on the letter AH in your throat, you can have experiences that are the manifestation of your subconscious mind becoming alive. Have these instructions been of help to you?

The fourth instruction you received allows you to be able to understand the instant between sleep and dream, and at this instant, the mind is present in its true nature with the experience of great clarity, which is more peaceful. This is the instruction on the luminous quality of the mind. Did this instruction benefit you?

You also received the fifth instruction through which you learned that at death consciousness has to leave the body. But if it leaves the body through one of the eight inferior apertures, the mind will go back to samsara. But if it goes through the ninth aperture,[34] it will follow the path that leads to Mahamudra realization. Did this instruction on phowa benefit you?

Finally, you also received a sixth instruction. This is the instruction that teaches you how to use the dream state to train for the *bardo* experiences so that during the bardo you can be liberated into the realization of the sambhogakaya or the nirmanakaya. Did this instruction on the bardo benefit you?

These six instructions you received are very special. They do not allow for any mistakes and won't lead you astray. These are the very highest instructions and you received them. So now you have no reason to be unhappy.

Then Naropa empowered Marpa as his representative and gave the great feast saying:

> Before, I had a special realization, and now you have gained this same realization that the five *aggregates* (Skt. *skandhas*) are the *five Buddha families* and that the five disturbing emotions are the *five wisdoms*. In the future, in Tibet, you will uphold both the teachings of the *sutras* and the tantras, but in particular you will shed the light of day on the Vajrayana teachings.
>
> Your family line will be broken, but your spiritual lineage will grow, more and more. For as long as the Buddha's teachings are present in this world, these teachings will never diminish. Some may look upon you as a man with many worldly attachments, but you know what the truth is because you have realized the true nature of phenomena.
>
> How others see you is like a coiled snake that looks like a knot. But all the snake needs to do is uncoil his body and the knot is gone all by itself. In the same way, from the outside it may look as though you are involved in worldly things. But because you understand the actual nature of phenomena, nothing can bind you. Everything automatically frees itself.

Naropa added that in the future Marpa's line of disciples would be very great and splendid. He said, "Your spiritual sons will be just like the *garudas*, and just like the snow lion, the offspring are better than the parents; the son will be better than the father and the son of the grandson will be better than his father. The next time we meet, we will always be together and never separate. So Marpa, don't be depressed, but rejoice and be very happy."

These words were actually spoken in prose, but he accompanied them with a spiritual song, which said about the same thing.

Marpa is Empowered

Naropa empowered Marpa as his representative. He predicted that in time Marpa would have a very strong and prosperous spiritual line in Tibet and that his disciples would become better and better as time went on so that this spiritual lineage would be like the stream of a very great river.

When Marpa received this empowerment as the representative of Naropa and received this prediction, he felt very happy. But at the same time he had mixed feelings about what was going to happen from then on. He still had to go back to Tibet and face all the hardships of the journey and this caused him to be unhappy and tense. Thinking of his guru and the dharma friends that he would leave behind, he felt sad. But then thinking of all the instructions and great teachings he was bringing back to Tibet, he again felt very happy.

So in this very mixed state of mind of being very happy and very sad, he sang a song of farewell to Naropa. He sang a song with a musical tune that imitated the humming of a swarm of bees far away:

The gurus are very kind to beings. But among all of them, the kindest is my guru, the mahapandita Naropa. He is a jewel that adorns my head.

And I, Marpa the Translator from Tibet, came to meet Naropa. The fact is that this meeting, here in India, was made possible by virtue and many prayers made in the past. Not only did we meet, but we stayed together for sixteen years and seven months. In all that time we were only apart from time to time. And during all that time together, our relationship was so very positive and beautiful. The guru never showed any displeasure or any dissatisfaction towards me. And I, the disciple, always tried to respect him as much as I could.

We stayed together in the monastery at Phullahari. At this monastery, Naropa gave me the complete four empowerments.

He also gave me the complete transmission of the instructions of the whispered lineage. Besides these instructions, I also practiced the superior means for achieving realization in one lifetime and came to realize the very nature of my mind.

Now I have to go back to Tibet. Since my guru has predicted that I will be able to help many beings and disciples, and since I have been appointed as his representative, I'm going with great joy.

But at the same time, there are three things that I will miss.

First, I shall miss all the great mahasiddhas who were my teachers, and most of all, Naropa and Maitripa. Now I have to leave them behind in India, but I shall keep on thinking of them and I will keep on missing them.

Second, I shall miss all my dharma brothers and sisters that I will leave behind in India, in particular my dharma friend Jigme Dragpa. Then there are all the other yogis and *yoginis* that I have to leave behind. But I will keep them in my mind and I will miss them.

Also I have to leave Phullahari behind, and all the other very special places where the mahasiddhas live. Now I have to leave them behind, but I will keep them in my mind and these too I will miss.

Marpa continued his song saying that there were three things that he feared on the way back to Tibet. The first thing was the great Ganges River.

It is very wide and very hard to cross, and even thinking of it now, I am afraid.

Then at the border between India and Nepal, there is a great mountain called the Usiri Mountain. This is a vast desert area where robbers and thieves wait in ambush there for people who travel. Even now, just thinking of it, I feel frightened.

Then at the border between Nepal and Tibet are the impossible custom's officials. They are so difficult to deal with that even now, just thinking of them, I feel frightened.

On the way to Tibet, on the road itself, there are three things that I am worried about.

The first will be the hundreds of very narrow and steep paths and bridges that I will have to go over. Just thinking of it now, I feel frightened.

Then there will be hundreds of very high passes that are extremely frigid. And just thinking of it now, I feel frightened.

Finally, there will be hundreds of very, very long and seemingly endless plains, one after the other. Just thinking of this, I feel frightened.

After the three reasons for being fearful, Marpa added the three reasons for feeling very happy:

The first reason is that, having learned everything about Sanskrit, I may be able to gather together many fellow translators,

The second reason for being glad is that, having studied hundreds of different tantras and their commentaries, particularly the Hevajra tantra and the Mahamaya tantra, I feel very happy at the thought of being able to gather many great scholars in Tibet to discuss these.

Finally, having received hundreds of instructions for practice, and particularly on the whispered transmission of the Mahamaya teaching, I feel very happy at the prospect of gathering many great meditators around me to teach these.

Then Marpa continued:

There are three very special things I have learned:

The first is that I received hundreds of instructions on the bardo. I received not just the sacred transmission of the teaching, but also the teaching enriched with all the instructions and all the commentaries, which can deepen the understanding of this practice. To have received this is really quite wonderful.

The second is that I received hundreds of teachings on the protectors who look after the Buddha's teaching. This is truly a wonderful thing.

The third special teachings that I received were all the profound instructions on Guhyasamaja and the five levels of the completion stage. Receiving hundreds of instructions on this is truly a wonderful thing.

Because of this, I feel truly, deeply happy. But how did I come to receive all these instructions? It was entirely due to the tremendous and deep kindness of my guru. Without my guru I couldn't have received any of these instructions. Presently, I am not able to repay such kindness. But later when I return to Tibet, I will spread all these teachings that have been given to me, and this will be my way to repay the great kindness of my guru.

Then Marpa prayed to Naropa to remain with him always, saying: "Please, always be above my head, and give me your blessing that I may not meet with any great difficulty or obstacles on my way back." And Marpa concluded, "I will not meet my guru or my dharma friends again in this lifetime. But I pray that later in the next lifetime, we may meet together in the pure land."

When Marpa had taken his leave from Naropa, he went to see Maitripa. From Maitripa, he received the Hevajra empowerment. And during this empowerment, a rain of heavenly flowers fell from space and a very exquisite scent of sandalwood arose from nowhere. There was a small fire of pinewood that burned for seven days without interruption, and very beautiful music could be heard coming from emptiness.

Following this, Maitripa gave Marpa the Chakrasamvara empowerment. During the empowerment, the songs of dakas and dakinis could be heard. At the point in the ceremony when one has to give the *tormas*, seven red wild animals appeared – manifestations of dakinis and protectors – to receive the torma offering. Finally, Maitripa said to Marpa, "Now you have received all these instructions, but they shouldn't be given to anybody in India."

7

Marpa in Tibet

Marpa returned to Tibet through Nepal and reached his home, concluding his third and final journey to India. This part of his biography relates that Marpa, through his very great intelligence, was able to introduce the most profound practices to realize the essential nature of phenomena.

In Tibet, Marpa spent his time doing practice. However, there were people who didn't have confidence in Marpa and said, "Well, he's just been to India, but in fact all he did there was to learn a lot of tricks. He is just deceiving us. In fact, he has not changed, he is just as negative as he ever was." So many bad things were being said that Marpa could see a very negative attitude developing toward what he was saying. In order to change their minds, he demonstrated some of the miracles that he had learned through Naropa's instructions.

To further eliminate the negative attitude affecting these people, he sang a spiritual song that clarified the various instructions he received from Naropa:

> I, Marpa Lotsawa, went to India and there I was able to receive all of the most profound teachings. I received the king of tantras, the Hevajra tantra. I was able to receive this from the great mahapandita Naropa himself. I also received all the teachings on Dentze and one particular aspect of this, which is the instruction on the ejection and transference of

consciousness. Also, I was given the instructions on dream meditation and the meditation on the great luminous clarity. I was given these instructions along with all the clarifying commentaries. Also, I was given the king of all the instructions for understanding the very nature of the mind, the subtle heat instruction. All this I received in India.

I was given the very precious instructions on gaining control of my prana. I also learned how to rid my body of sickness and disease. I learned that my body was the very mandala of the deity, and I was given instructions on how to develop and increase the power of my vital energy and all the systems that convey this vital energy in my body.

Now all of you who feel distrust toward me, and do not like who I am or what I have done, can appreciate the value of what I received. You no longer need this lack of trust and confidence.

Once they heard this, most felt very great respect for what Marpa had received. They realized that these were the very profound teachings of the tantras. As a result, they began to realize the value of these teachings and felt a great desire to practice them. With this doha many of his students were able to practice productively.

After Chapter Seven in the original text there is a very interesting example by Marpa of how we should study the dharma. It says:

Once upon a time in India there was a small island that was a few days journey away from the continent by sailboat. Many people used to travel to this island because it was famous for containing very precious things such as diamonds and gold. Many people went there, but they had to face a lot of difficulties such as great storms and other dangers to go there.

Imagine going to great length to journey there, facing hardships all the way, and upon arriving on the island, forgetting why we went to the island. If we forgot, we would never find jewels or gold, and would go back empty-handed. We would be a fool for wasting this great opportunity after putting so much effort into it. When we had come to our senses we would have to go back again to get the jewels.

In the same way, we now have a great opportunity when all the jewels are before us. All we have to do is to remember them. This is our great chance. If we think "Well, maybe I'll do it later," we may well never get the opportunity to do so again. So we should use the opportunity now without being careless or inattentive, because it is our great chance.

Throughout all our activities we should make certain to not be lazy and careless. Whether we are receiving teachings or meditating or reciting mantras or making prayers, we should do it as carefully and as properly as we can without thinking, "It's not very important." What we must do is to direct our mind, body and speech to the direction of the dharma; put our whole self into the practice and think to ourselves this is what we want to do right now. And if we do this, then we will, of course, attain the goal of our diligent efforts.

In one of Milarepa's poems it is said that laziness is our enemy. It is like the deep sleep of a corpse, a rest that is of no benefit to anyone at all. Laziness persuades us that it might be very nice to let ourselves not do anything, which appears to be a very pleasant course of action. But really, it is a very shortsighted view because in the long term, this attitude hurts us and actually makes living much more difficult. Milarepa continues on, saying, "Laziness is a major obstacle. It is an obstacle which will prevent us from practicing properly." In other words, laziness prevents us from reducing our suffering. If we believe that this is a major obstacle, we must do everything we can to reject it.

8

How Marpa Lost His Son

n the previous chapter, we were told that Marpa established his practice in Tibet. We know from the earlier chapters that although Marpa had seven sons, his family line wouldn't continue, but that his dharma line would be very great. This next part of the story deals with these events related to Marpa's son, Darmadode. The death of Darmadode led to the termination of several important transmissions that Marpa had brought back from India, namely, the four instructions on the ejection of consciousness and the instructions on re-entering the body. With this obstacle of the death of Darmadode, the teachings for the ejection of consciousness did not develop in Tibet as many of the other teachings had and these practices have been rarely used and it became impossible for these teachings to develop and be practiced in Tibet.

The death of Darmadode was, of course, very tragic for Marpa, his wife, and his disciples. Although the event itself was extremely painful, it had one positive result of instilling a very deep sense of renunciation in all those who were left behind. Marpa had seven sons and, of these, six displayed no great intelligence, courage, or compassion. They were like anyone else. However, his son Darmadode, was quite extraordinary.

Before Marpa left India for the last time, Naropa advised Marpa to spend three years in retreat with his son and to give him the full transmission of all the instructions that he had received. So Marpa and his son went into retreat in the town of Lhotrak. While they were in retreat there was a very special festival being celebrated nearby. Some people came to Marpa's house and invited Marpa to come, and if he couldn't, they invited his son, insisting that one of them should come. Marpa's wife told the guests that based on Naropa's advice, they had to stay in retreat together for three years, so they couldn't go to the festival, but that one of Marpa's close disciples could be sent.

Negative forces, however, were working directly on Darmadode and he suddenly began to develop an urge to go to the festival. He felt that he was in the prime of his life and that the event would be the highlight of his youth. Since he was young and in good health, he thought, "Why shouldn't I go to the festival and enjoy myself?" The urge to go grew stronger in him and that night he dreamt of an old woman holding a stake in her hands, saying that she was on her way to the festival because she really wanted to go. Darmadode thought, "Well, if even that old hag wants to go, and since I am much younger than her, I should go and have a good time there also."

The next day he told his parents that he really wanted to go to the festival. Of course, his parents knew that it might not be the right thing to do and didn't want him to go. But they finally conceded, saying, "Well, if you go, there are several things that you really must not do at any cost." They told him that first he shouldn't sit in the main seat, which in Tibet is the first row near all the action. Also, he shouldn't teach dharma. Finally, he shouldn't drink any alcohol or do any horse racing. So they said, "If you agree, then you may go." Darmadode agreed and went.

When Darmadode arrived at the festival, people began to ask, "Who is that man?" When they found out it was the great Marpa's son they said, "Oh, please, you must come and sit here at the head row." So they sat him in the best seat. Once Darmadode was seated there, some people said, "Well, you should tell us a little bit about dharma, maybe say a few things." And of course, he got talking and started saying many things. After so much talking he became thirsty.

Somebody came around and offered him some beer. He had a little bit here and a little bit there, and by the end he drank quite a lot. His uncle, who was at the festival, had an excellent horse. The people all said, "Well, you must try the horse. You are very good at spiritual things, but it's not enough to be a spiritual expert. You should also try to develop some physical abilities and show us what you can do at horse racing." They continued, "You really must try that horse." Darmadode remembered what his parents had said and thought, "I can't go." But at the same time everything was carrying him towards the race, so he said, "Okay, I'll try it."

At that point, Marpa's student Milarepa who was also attending the festival realized that Darmadode was really getting very carried away and that he had disobeyed several of his parents' instructions, so he said to Darmadode, "Come on, let's go back now. It's better to go back."

But Darmadode went on to ride the horse. By that time he had too much to drink and couldn't really handle the mount. The horse was still tied by a rope, and so he said to the others, "You ride ahead and I will catch up with you." The others went ahead. Darmadode mounted and began to ride when a startled bird suddenly screamed the way a crow may loudly caw as it flies by. The horse spooked badly, reared up, and threw Darmadode to the ground where he hit his head. It was said that when his parents came his head was broken into eight pieces.

Darmadode's mother asked Marpa if he could do something because he was very skilled in medical science. Marpa had to admit that he couldn't do anything, but he said to his son, "Please do not forget your instructions." But at that point, Darmadode was already quite far-gone, moving in and out of consciousness.

Marpa had great hope that his son would carry on his teachings and thus help so many beings to accomplish liberation. Now he was extremely sad and distressed. At that same time, there was a couple in the town whose child had recently died and they were still suffering a great deal. Marpa had advised them that death was just the nature of phenomena in samsara; samsara was like a magical illusion or a dream. The death of their child should be viewed like the death of a child who is born and dies in the course of a dream. When this couple heard that Marpa's son had died, they came to see him and said very respectfully, "But this death of your son also is merely a dream, a magical illusion." And Marpa replied, "That is true. But among dreams this is a very great dream and among illusions, this is a great illusion." Then he added, "I'm not suffering because it is painful to me to be separated from my son and I'm not suffering because I'm afraid that he's going to the *lower realms.* I'm suffering because his death is a tremendous impediment to the vast benefit for beings and the teachings of the Buddha." Because of the realization of Marpa and the realization of Darmadode, this adverse situation was not a particular problem for them personally. Darmadode, while moving in and out of consciousness, said, "There is no need to be so sad." And he was able to sing this spiritual song:

> Everyone must die someday. But now, through the very great kindness of my father Marpa, I will not have any suffering when I die because of the instructions he gave me. So I do not have any worry about dying. My only worry is that I will be unable to repay the great kindness of my father and mother. My dying request to my parents is 'please do not be upset.' I haven't forgotten the instructions that my dear father has given me: the teachings on the tantras and their commentaries and the teachings of the Six Yogas of Naropa. They are all present, completely alive in my mind. I have no fear of the bardo or what will happen in my future life.
>
> And now I make a prayer that in the next life, we may all be able to meet in a pure land.

Since Darmadode possessed the instructions for the ejection of consciousness, and for transferring one's consciousness into a corpse and resuscitating the corpse, he asked the other disciples of Marpa to go and find a corpse for him. So they went in search of a corpse, but they couldn't find anything suitable. All they found in the cemetery was a little baby's body. The parents became upset when they saw the child's body moving and thought that a ghost was taking possession of it. They became frightened and blinded its eyes with needles. So Marpa's son did not enter the corpse. Because Darmadode did not enter another human body the instructions of ejection of consciousness and resuscitation did not develop in Tibet.

Later, Marpa's son transferred his consciousness into the corpse of a pigeon, and flew to India and alighted in the cemetery of Sitavana or "Cool Grove." There he found and entered the body of a child of a Brahmin family. When the dead body rose and started walking, people working in the cemetery were terrified. Fortunately Darmadode could speak some of the local language and said, "Don't worry, I'm not a ghost. I'm just someone who's come back to life!"

Then the people working in the cemetery were most impressed. They took the child to the parents and the parents were overjoyed because their son was back. Later, of course, they realized that their son wasn't quite the same. He seemed to possess qualities that their son had never had before, and his way of thinking was quite different from their son's and that their son was now quite extraordinary. So they asked him all sorts of questions and the child told them the whole story. He told them that he had transferred his consciousness into the body of a pigeon, and then from the body of a pigeon into the corpse of their son. That is when he was given the name of Tiphupa, which means "the pigeon one."

In the meantime, back in Tibet, everybody was extremely saddened by what had happened. Darmadode's mother, Dagmema, and Marpa and all the disciples deeply grieved the death of Darmadode.[35] It came to such a painful point that Marpa sang a song to try to dissipate their grief. He sang:

Yes, we have lost Darmadode who was a very exceptional son,
but we have to understand that everything in the world and

life is like this. Everything is just an illusion. The death of Darmadode should illustrate this to us very clearly. It is part of the very nature of conditioned existence that things cease, and this is a very clear example to us. So we shouldn't grieve.

Far more important for us to do is to practice the dharma. We possess the rarest and most precious jewels of the teaching. We have all of the whispered lineage instructions and we have all the teachings of the tantras. So although we have lost Darmadode, we must put these teachings to use.

Naropa had predicted that my family line would be broken. But he also predicted that my spiritual lineage would be very strong and very great. So what we have to do now is to work for what will be very beneficial for all sentient beings, not only in the short term, but also for the very long term.

When Marpa had spoken in this way, his wife Dagmema and all his disciples felt a very, very strong sense of renunciation, and also developed a very deep wish to practice as sincerely as possible. They all started practicing from that time on with very great and intense diligence.

In Marpa's biography, the story of the great suffering of Marpa and Dagmema and their students at the time of the death of Darmadode is recorded and given to be an example of how we should deal with our own situations as practitioners. Although we meet great gurus and receive extraordinary instructions, we nevertheless encounter obstacles and extremely adverse conditions. When obstacles and suffering arise, we find ourselves thinking: "Why is this happening to me? I'm a practitioner, this shouldn't be happening," and we start to blame ourselves. We begin to think that something is wrong with our practice. This can happen to a single individual or it can happen to an entire spiritual community. What is important to understand is that the appearance of obstacles is not contradictory to the path of dharma. With the dharma we can actually overcome obstacles and by overcoming obstacles we mean that we are actually trained to the point that these obstacles neither harm us in our practice nor in our worldly affairs.

How the Teachings of Marpa Spread

One day Marpa and some of his disciples were together and some of his main disciples asked Marpa what would happen to the Kagyu tradition. They said, "Now that your son, the great bodhisattva Darmadode, is no longer with us and you are getting older, we are wondering how the teachings of this oral transmission lineage will be transmitted in the future."

Marpa reiterated that Naropa had predicted that his family line would stop, but that his spiritual line would develop and be very strong. So he said, "In order to see exactly what's going to happen in the future, I would like all of you to be attentive to the dreams you are going to have tonight."

Among their dreams, Milarepa had one that was particularly significant. Milarepa told his dream in the form of a spiritual song:

Following my guru's request, I looked at my dreams and this is what I saw.

In the middle of Tibet, I saw a very high snow mountain that was pointing right into the sky. On either side of this mountain peak were the sun and the moon. Then to the east I saw a great pillar and on top of the pillar was standing a lion. The lion had a very thick and very beautiful mane. He was gazing into space. Then the lion jumped onto the mountain.

To the south, I saw another pillar on which a tiger stood and the tiger was roaring very, very loudly. He had very beautiful fur arranged with very beautiful designs. Then the tiger jumped into a forest.

On the western side was another pillar on which was standing a garuda. The garuda had great wings and feathers and was gazing into space as it flew into the sky.

On the northern side there was another pillar where a vulture stood. I saw the vulture giving birth to young ones, and then these gave birth to others, so that in the end, the whole of the sky was filled with vultures. In the end they built a nest on the rock.

When Milarepa finished telling his dream, he said, "This is what I saw, and I feel this might be a good dream, but would the lama be kind enough to interpret the dream and say whether this was good or bad."

Marpa interpreted the dream in this way:

The snow mountain is myself, Marpa. And the fact that it was very great indicates the great development of the Kagyu teaching. That it goes right into the sky shows that the Mahamudra view is very profound. The sun and the moon on either side of the mountain signify the very brilliant clarity of the mind that can be experienced in meditation.

Each of the pillars represents one of my main disciples. The eastern pillar represents Dorje Tsultrim and the lion on the pillar shows that Dorje Tsultrim has the qualities of a lion that is completely fearless; the qualities of his practice are excellent and incomparable with anyone else.

The southern pillar represents my other disciple, Ngoktön Chödor. The tiger on the pillar represents his tiger-like quality, and the very clear and beautiful fur on his body shows that he will keep the instructions of the whispered lineage very clear and unspoiled.

The western pillar represents Meton Tsonpo, and his particular quality is garuda-like. The fact that he flew into the sky shows that his view will be as great and vast as the sky.

The northern pillar represents my other disciple Milarepa, and he has particularly vulture-like qualities. The fact that the vulture[36] was giving birth to baby vultures shows that he will have very excellent disciples. The vultures filling the whole of space signifies that his teachings will fill the whole world, spreading everywhere and that he will have many very, very excellent disciples, some being better than the master. And then the disciples of those previous disciples will be even better, so that the line will become better and better. The fact that the vultures in the dream alighted on a rock and built their nest on the rock signifies that Milarepa will have a very long life without any obstacles to his longevity.

Following this revelation, the disciples of Marpa practiced all their instructions with even greater care. They had always respected the instructions, but now their diligence was reinforced and they practiced very intensively day and night.

Marpa then started wondering how to distribute the various instructions among his main disciples so that in the future people would benefit in the best possible way. He considered who should receive this particular instruction and who should receive that one. He decided to examine the signs that could indicate to him who was the best possible person for the transmission of each set of teachings.

One morning he examined the signs. In his meditation he looked at what each one of his main disciples was doing at that particular moment. What he saw was a very strong indication of how he should pass on the teachings. Marpa saw that Ngoktör Chödor was engaged in the study and practice of the commentary of the Hevajra tantra. He saw that at the same time Dorje Tsultrim Wangnge was practicing the ejection of consciousness. He saw that Meton Tsonpo was practicing the instructions on the brilliant clarity of the mind, and, finally, he saw that Milarepa was practicing tummo. This then was an indication to him who would specialize in each particular aspect of the teachings. He decided to give each one the instructions on the teaching that they were practicing at the time he had examined the signs.

Having decided this, Marpa proceeded to give the various instructions to each of the four main disciples. To Ngoktör Chödor he gave the full instructions on the Hevajra and the Chakrasamvara tantra. These were not just the usual ritual reading or empowerment, but were the very precise and extensive instructions on the tantra in all its various forms. To help his progress in these practices and to support his *samaya* commitment to do these practices, Marpa presented Chödor with the six bone ornaments of Naropa together with Naropa's ruby rosary and Marpa's own copies of the original tantras. Marpa said to him, "Your particular way of helping beings in the future will be through explaining the tantras. So try to do your best in explaining them."

To his disciple Tsultrim Wangnge, he gave the complete set of phowa or ejection of consciousness instructions. As a token of his specialization in the phowa practice, he gave him some hair of Naropa and the crown of five pieces made of bones that Naropa used to wear on his head. He then said to him, "Your particular way of helping beings will be through the ejection of consciousness instructions. So please do your best in that direction."

Then to Meton Tsonpo he gave all the instructions on luminosity, the great clarity of the mind. To help him with mastering these teachings, he presented him with the vajra, bell, and *dharmaru* that had belonged to Naropa. Marpa also asked Meton to spread the teachings on the bardo.

Finally, he gave Milarepa all the instructions on tummo practice. As a sign of Milarepa's specialization in that teaching, he presented him with the clothes of Naropa – an auspicious sign for his realization of the view of Mahamudra – and gave him the hat that had belonged to Maitripa. Marpa told Milarepa to go and live in solitary places, and practice tummo instructions until he had achieved full realization of the view and the meditation with the instructions, "This is how you will be able to help all beings."

After Marpa had given the various teachings, most of the disciples went to their own residences to practice. But Marpa told Milarepa to remain for a short period of time. Although Marpa had given all of his instructions to all of his close disciples, in accordance with Naropa's prophecy, he gave Milarepa the special empowerments, transmissions and instructions for the oral lineage of Chakrasamvara, which was governed by a command seal.[37]

9

Marpa Teaches Through Miracles

In the third part of the biography it shows how, through very great realization, Marpa was able to do all sorts of miracles showing that he had the highest realization. Marpa did miracles to inspire confidence in the path for his students and so even ordinary people could see the signs of Marpa's great realization.

The most remarkable miracle of Marpa can still be experienced today. This is the extraordinary spiritual line to which he gave birth. Think of all the people who have been able to achieve ultimate realization since Marpa's time and then how many more were able to achieve some spiritual accomplishment, and how many people just began practicing because of Marpa. This in itself is a very special achievement that we could say is a miracle of Marpa's realization.

The very special quality of these teachings of Marpa's is that they truly can explain to others how to accomplish realization. We learn from these teachings that it is possible to give up our negative emotions and to actually attain true freedom from suffering. Much of the time this seems very far away, almost impossible to achieve. We usually experience our disturbing emotions as being so deeply ingrained in our mind that to attain clarity of mind seems hopeless. But with the very special instructions that have been transmitted to us from Marpa through his lineage, it is actually possible to eliminate these emotions that disturb us.

There are two basic aspects of spiritual accomplishment: the ordinary aspect and the supreme aspect, which is complete realization. Once we know that there were very great masters who achieved this, then we see that it is quite possible for us to accomplish these goals also. The very profound teachings that they passed on to us are what puts accomplishment within our grasp and makes it possible to actually realize it ourselves. While it seems so far away, and once may have been, it is Marpa's teaching through miracles that actually narrowed this seemingly great gap.

When we speak of Marpa's miracles, we may refer to the miracles that he performed physically or those such as clairvoyance, which he performed through the power of his mind. But in fact, the greatest and most remarkable miracle of all was that he was able to show so many other beings the possibility of accomplishing realization.

Marpa passed away almost a thousand years ago, but we still have his teachings. It is the direct result of his activity that we can still practice the very profound teachings of the Six Yogas of Naropa, the Mahamudra instructions, and so on. So depending on our diligence and energy, we may achieve any level of spiritual accomplishment. This spiritual accomplishment is not just the understanding of the words and concepts of the practice, but the ability to personally experience what it actually means to be free of the negative emotions and to truly understand the nature of reality. All of this was made possible through Marpa's enlightened action and this is why it is his greatest miracle.

Miracles that can be physically created will inspire people who see them to have more faith and devotion, but the effect of such miracles are temporary. In contrast, the supreme "miracle of speech" has endless results. From the time that the teachings were first given until the time when the Buddha's teachings disappear from the face of the earth, these teachings will be available for anyone to practice and to accomplish the fruition.

The miracle of speech surpasses all other kinds of miracles because its effect will not end for as long as the Buddha's teachings are present.

In fact the oral transmission of these teachings not only remains but also continues to expand, more and more.

This doesn't imply that Marpa was only capable of doing this supreme type of miracle, because it is quite clear from his biography that he also performed quite remarkable "ordinary miracles." Even Milarepa had several experiences of Marpa's miracles. Sometimes, when Milarepa came to see Marpa, he found him in the form of one of the deities. Sometimes he didn't see anything at all because his body was totally invisible. At other times Milarepa saw him in the form of brilliant lights and rainbows. Whenever Marpa showed him this type of miracle, he would ask Milarepa, "Did you see my miracle? Did you believe in it?" And Milarepa would answer, "Yes, I can see you are a very special lama and I did see your miracle. And I can't help believing in it."

Marpa also displayed miracles to his other disciples from time to time. Marpa Golek sometimes saw Marpa in the form of Hevajra. Sometimes he and others saw him in the form of Chakrasamvara, or of Guhyasamaja or Vajravarahi. When some of Marpa's disciples saw him in these various forms, they asked him questions such as, "Why did we see you in the form of Hevajra or Chakrasamvara?" Marpa would answer something like, "Well, it is likely that you saw me like this because at the time, I was visualizing this particular deity. But at this same time, you must also have been feeling very open and full of trust towards me, and the meeting of these two things at the same moment produces this kind of vision."

Some other disciples didn't see Marpa in the form of various deities or yidams, but they did see very unusual things. Sometimes where Marpa had been sitting they would see a large fire or they would see very clear water or they would see rainbows, or they would see nothing at all except for a brilliant light. These students would then ask Marpa why they were seeing these things by saying, "We do not see you in the form of a yidam, but we see clear water or fire or light. What does that mean? Does this mean that we are impure or pure?" Marpa, in one of his spiritual songs explained that when someone is undergoing a process of purification, there is a transformation of the whole system whereby the subtle inner channels and all the vital winds or energy that circulates in them have to undergo a complete process of purification. While this process of transformation is taking place, it is possible to see the raw elements as they had seen them.

In our body, we have a central channel, and within that there is a circulation of energy taking place. These vital energies propel bodhichitta, the vital energy. When we practice meditation and particularly when we do the tummo practice in combination with the various postures and movements of this practice, our mind is in a state of very great clarity. At that point, it is possible for those who have developed enough spiritually to see these things such as light, fire, rainbows and so on.

Sometimes when Marpa was inside the room and the doors and the windows were closed, he could be seen walking through the walls as if there were nothing there. One of his sons used to make jokes about this saying, "Oh, if you were a thief it would be really convenient because you could just come and go without being stopped by walls or anything."

So this was a very brief account of Marpa's miracles by way of his pure body, speech and mind. Only a brief account was given because what is most important is the teachings that Marpa left to us which we can experience ourselves. The other miracles won't make a tremendous difference to our faith because our faith can be aroused and developed from Marpa's teachings.

This concludes the third section of Marpa's life story.

10

Marpa's Passing into Nirvana

*T*he fourth section of the biography of Marpa tells us how Marpa passed away. The actual title of this short section of Marpa's spiritual biography, or *namtar*, is "How, after Marpa worked for the sake of the teachings and all beings, his body dissolved into the *dharmadhatu.*" In its description of Marpa's death, this chapter fulfills the literal meaning of *namtar* in Tibetan, "full liberation."

The time of Marpa's passing was at dawn on the fifteenth day of the first Tibetan month of the year when the sun was just reaching the top of a nearby mountain. Marpa was 88 years old. He wasn't sick at all and felt tremendously happy and joyful. He told one of his disciples, Marpa Golek, to prepare many beautiful offerings. Looking incredibly happy and smiling, he folded his hands at his heart as we do when we make an offering and said, "Now I can go and join Naropa and all the dakas and dakinis." And then he passed away just sitting in meditation. It is said that when he passed away, many very beautiful things appeared. The sky suddenly filled with rainbows and a rain of flowers fell. Very unusual divine music could be heard and very beautiful fragrant scents could be smelled. From the crown of his head, a five-colored light radiated and filled the whole sky, then his wife Dagmema dissolved into light and melted into him. This was how Marpa passed away.

We have reached the end of Marpa's biography, and it is important to remember that Marpa appeared to most people as a very ordinary man. It was only to his very close disciples who were spiritually ready to understand, that he performed miracles and did special things.

Marpa had thirteen gurus in India with the main ones being Naropa, Maitripa, Kukkuripa, and Yeshe Nyingpo. He had seven sons. But of his sons only one of them was really important in terms of the dharma, and that was his son Darmadode. The others didn't do anything outstanding in connection with the dharma. Thus Naropa's prediction that he would have no family line, but a very strong line of spiritual sons was correct. Marpa had eight main disciples, four of whom were called the "four pillars of the teachings," and four who had a special connection with Marpa from a past lifetime, called the "four with a karmic link."

The Chakrasamvara Tradition of the Trungpa Lineage

We might view this biography from the point of view of how Marpa was born, what he studied, how he practiced, what he taught, and the circumstances surrounding his passing away. However, if we look beyond ordinary appearances, we discover that before Marpa was born, he was the Indian siddha known as Dombhi Heruka, which is mentioned briefly in Marpa's biography. This siddha performed such actions as riding around on a tiger and using a poisonous snake as a riding crop. Following that lifetime, he was reborn as Marpa, and then after that lifetime he was reborn again in Tibet as Trungmase Lodro Rinchen who was a student of the Fifth Karmapa, Deshin Shekpa. The Karmapa at one point made the statement that of the many profound lineages that he held, the most profound lineage was that of Chakrasamvara. The Karmapa presented this lineage to Trungmase Lodro Rinchen to keep and protect. The lineage of the Trungpa tulkus are the emanations of the body, speech, and mind of Trungmase Lodro Rinchen.

So, although we've talked about the external circumstances of Marpa's life, what we're really talking about is Trungpa Rinpoche. Among all the instructions in the gradual format that have been presented to the students of Trungpa Rinpoche,[38] the final, or ultimate, instruction of his presentation has been the empowerment and sadhana of Chakrasamvara.

This was the innermost path of Naropa's instructions entrusted to Marpa, and again entrusted by the Fifth Gyalwa Karmapa to Trungmase Lodro Rinchen. Since then it has passed primarily through the lineage of the Trungpas.[39]

How the Biography was Written

The way this biography came to be written was that some of Marpa's disciples, such as Milarepa and Marpa Golek, had made some notes on Marpa's life and these notes were used by a great mahasiddha who then wrote the biography. In Tibet there were three very famous mahasiddhas who were called "madmen." There was the Madman of Tsang, The Madman of Druk and the Madman of central Tibet. It was the Madman of Tsang, named Tsang Nyön Heruka, who used these notes to compile this biography of Marpa.

Concluding Statement

Marpa has passed away and there is nothing left of him outwardly, but his all-seeing mind and his pure intelligence is still here. Whenever we do anything positive and negative with our body, speech or mind, Marpa can see all of it as clearly as if it were in the palm of his hand.

There is something else we should also consider. Marpa went through very many difficulties to obtain teachings for the sake of all beings so that he naturally remains concerned with the way the teachings are being practiced as well as the welfare and progress of those who are practicing them. He wants to see whether or not they are doing things properly, whether or not they are able to reduce their negative emotions and whether or not they are gaining some understanding. One could say that his hopes concerning the quality of the practice of disciples are in proportion to the great hardships that he went through to receive these teaching. If Marpa sees that we can't do that or that we don't take the trouble to do it, then he feels very saddened.

We shouldn't believe that when we do things, it makes no difference because no one is aware of it. Not only Marpa, but all the Buddhas and bodhisattvas are aware of our behavior. Everything we do, they can see and understand very clearly. So, we should out of respect for their complete knowledge of our actions, words, and thoughts try to act as purely as possible. Keeping Marpa's teachings in mind, we should always try to act and think and speak in the best possible way.

Notes

1. The Tibetan words are given as they are pronounced, not spelled in Tibetan. For their actual spelling see the Glossary of Tibetan words.
2. *The Life of Marpa the Translator* by Tsang Nyön Heruka and translated by the Nalanda Translation Committee. Boston: Shambhala Publications, 1986.
3. *The Life of Marpa the Translator: Seeing Accomplishes All* (Tib. *ra byur mar pa lo tsa namtar tong ba don yod*).
4. Shariputra was one of the main arhat disciples of the Buddha.
5. The Buddhist belief about reality is different from our ordinary view. Normally we believe that the objects outside of us such as trees and rocks and people are solid, fairly unchanging and real. However, Buddhists believe that external phenomena are actually empty and have the nature of illusion. To give an example, if we and all our friends look at a chair, we all see it as solid, made of wood, and brown in color. However, physicists will tell us that actually the chair is really made up of 99.99% space with atoms, which cannot be located in any specific place, moving at incredible speeds and flying off all the time. Not only that but the wood is actually composed of atoms of carbon, hydrogen and oxygen, and the brown color is simply a wavelength of radiation that human (not animal) eyes see as "brown." Thrangu Rinpoche gives the example of Milarepa who actually realized the true empty nature of external objects and was therefore able to do things such as put his hand through rocks.
6. Disturbing emotions are kleshas which in Sanskrit means "pain, distress, and torment." This was translated as "afflictions" which is the closest English word to what causes distress. However, the Tibetan word for kleshas is *nyon mong* and these almost always refer to passion, anger, ignorance, jealousy, and pride which are actually negative or disturbing emotions so we prefer the translation negative or disturbing emotion since "afflictions" imply some kind of disability.

The Great Tibetan Dictionary for example defines *nyon mong* as, "mental events that incite one to non-virtuous actions and cause one's being to be very unpeaceful."

7. This event occurred in Parping in Nepal and today there is a Hindu Vihara (with a Vajrayogini statue that Marpa is said to have meditated in front of) where this is said to have occurred.

8. This "connection by previous relationship" is a type of a link that persons have with a lama, which is not a relationship in terms of cause and effect (karmic results), but comes out of a previous relationship. It comes from a habit of the past. For example, if, in the past, a lama had a disciple who received his or her instructions, worked with them, had faith in them and aspired to be with them to continue to receive teachings, this kind of relationship could take form again. This will then create a very strong cause for such a student and such a lama to come together to give and receive these teachings again.

   So a task that began jointly was unfinished, and yet contained within it the desire to carry on such a relationship to completion. It's like starting a joke and not quite finishing the joke and wanting to continue until it's completely told. So a disciple's relationship with a given lama leaves a very strong imprint in the subconscious and then, in the next lifetime, their subconscious memory suddenly wakes up and then one wants to again be with and receive teachings from that particular lama. – *Thrangu Rinpoche*

9. The tantras have been classified into four broad groups: The Kriya tantra (translated as the "action tantra"), the Carya tantra (translated as "performance tantra"), the Yoga tantra (or "union tantra") and the highest Anuttarayoga tantra ("unsurpassed union tantra"). The Anuttarayoga tantra, often called just the Anuttara tantra, is considered the highest set of tantras. (See *Guhyasamaja tantra, father tantra, Hevajra tantra, mother tantra*)

10. In the Tibetan system there are subtle energies (Skt. *prana*, Tib. *lung*) that move along subtle channels (Skt. *nadi*, Tib. *tsa*) that are not anatomical, but more like the meridians in acupuncture. In the higher tantric practices there are exercises that are designed to initiate these processes and move these energies along their pathways so that they make the practice go better.

11. In the Vajrayana, there are two paths – *drol lam* and *thap lam* – that are generally followed simultaneously or alternately by the practitioner. *Drol lam*, the path of liberation, is what sometimes we refer to as formless meditation and includes Mahamudra. In this approach to meditation one relates to the mind in terms of the awareness aspect of mind.

Thap lam, the path of means or method, includes all tantric practices employing visualization, mantras, mandalas, yogas such as *the Six Dharmas of Naropa* or the *Six Dharmas of Niguma,* etc. These practices relate to mind in terms of the energy aspect of mind. By properly integrating the distorted karmic energies of one's mind, one brings about the same enlightened awareness that is reached as the fruition of the formless meditation approach of the path of liberation. The virtue of the path of liberation is that it tends to be smoother, while the path of means is that it tends to be faster; therefore, they make a good complement to each other. Neither path can be practiced properly – and in the case of the path of means it would be dangerous to do so – without the guidance of a qualified tantric master. – *Lama Tashi Namgyal*

12. Vajradhara (Tib. *Dorje Chang*) is the dharmakaya of the Buddha. Tilopa, who was an emanation of Chakrasamvara, received these teachings by visiting a dakini in the sambhoga-kaya realm.

13. *Chanting the Names of Manjushri* (Skt *Manjushri Nama Sangiti*) has been translated by Alex Wayman and "is probably the most revered and recited tantric text among all the Tibetan Buddhist sects." (p. 28).

14. Saraha is known as the forefather of the Mahamudra lineage and his spiritual songs have been translated by Herbert Guenther in *Ecstatic Spontaneity - Saraha's Three Cycles of Doha.*

15. This is Niguma who was Naropa's sister. She was one of the great tantric practitioners and went on to teach the Six Yogas of Niguma which became an important part of the Shangpa Kagyu sect. Kalu Rinpoche was the head of the Shangpa sect before he passed away.

16. *The Rain of Wisdom* is a collection of works of the profound songs of great teachers of the Kagyu lineage. They were composed spontaneously by these masters and express their spiritual understanding. They have been translated by the Nalanda Translation Committee as *The Rain of Wisdom, The Essence of the Ocean of True Meaning.* Shambhala Publications, 1999.

17. Tilopa was founder of the Kagyu lineage and teacher of Naropa. Naropa's twelve ordeals are described in Guenther's *The Life and Teachings of Naropa.* Oxford: Oxford University Press, 1963.

18. We prefer to use the word emptiness instead of voidness because voidness implies just the absence of anything. Whereas the emptiness of shunyata is the absence of an inherent nature, which means that on the ultimate level of reality things do not exist, but on a relative level they do appear.

19. The Buddha's mind is the dharmakaya, but ordinary beings, because they have many disturbing emotions and false views of the nature of reality, cannot communicate directly with the dharmakaya. So the Buddha appears as the sambhogakaya, which is a pure realm that can be visited by highly realized beings (Buddhas and bodhisattvas) to receive teachings. In fact, Tilopa visited one of these realms to receive teachings. Finally, ordinary beings must rely on a human to receive teachings, and this is the nirmanakaya, with the Shakyamuni Buddha being the "supreme nirmanakaya." Clearly, if the Buddha had little compassion to help other beings he would not manifest as the sambhogakaya and nirmanakaya. However due to his compassion these two forms appear spontaneously wherever needed.

20. It is important to understand that the term prajna includes in one term the notions of knowledge, wisdom, and primordial awareness or transcendental awareness, which is the highest form of prajna. Worldly knowledge – medicine, literature, business management, economics or anthropology – is one form of prajna. Knowledge of the teachings of the Buddha and other enlightened beings is spiritual prajna. Both worldly and spiritual prajna are based on the acquisition of information, and though they may have a great deal of practical benefit, they will not by themselves liberate one from the root causes of suffering. Only the highest form of prajna, jnana – primordial awareness, which is liberated from the superimposition on experience of perceiver and perceived – will free one from the root causes of suffering. – *Lama Tashi Namgyal*

21. The literal word in Tibetan is "hearing," because in earlier times one's instructions came mostly from hearing explanations by the guru. But Thrangu Rinpoche has said that this means more like studying because many of these instructions are written down.

22. Blessing is the process by which one individual introduces some of their accumulated merit into another's "stream of being." The ability to bestow blessing depends on the donor's degree of spiritual attainment and on the recipient's faith. The donor is usually the root-guru, whose blessing is said to contain that of all the sources of refuge combined. Although future experiences are largely shaped by present actions, the root-guru's blessing can partially modify this. That is, it can create conditions favourable to the maturation of any religious pre-dispositions our past actions may have generated, giving us the inspiration and energy we require to begin practising. In this way, unless our acts have been extremely unwholesome, the guru's blessing can help us

overcome conflicting emotions and other obstacles. Thus the guru's blessing helps us realize the Buddha-potential we all possess.

23. Praying in the Buddhist context does not imply praying for intercession or propitiation. When we pray to receive blessings in Buddhism, we are praying that we will open up our mind to receive the energy created by the great masters of the lineage.

24. Yidam meditation is a meditation in which one visualizes a deity such as Padmasambhava or Avalokiteshvara or Tara. In this Vajrayana practice, called a sadhana, one creates the deity through visualization and does the practice and in the end one dissolves the deity (usually into oneself) to represent the inseparability of the deity and oneself.

25. In fact Nyö Lotsawa was so jealous when he realized that Marpa knew more than he did that he bribed a boatman to throw all of Marpa's texts in the river. However, Marpa had learned most of these texts by heart so they were not lost.

26. Placing something on one's head is a sign of respect. Tibetans will usually touch a Buddhist text or picture to the top of their head after looking at it.

27. Ordinary mind (Tib. *thamel gyi shepa*) is the original mind, or mind's natural state, before disturbing emotions and misconceptions about reality mask it. It is not the mind as we ordinarily think of with all its thoughts and confusions.

28. When you talk about guru in the Mahamudra lineage, there is the pure (dharmakaya) aspect of the guru, the distance lineage gurus, and the close lineage gurus. The distance lineage gurus start with the Lord Buddha and extend in a continuous, unbroken succession of enlightened masters and students all the way down to the Karmapa. We call that the distance lineage because it goes all the way back to the Buddha Shakyamuni.

There is the close lineage of Mahamudra as well. That lineage begins with the Buddha Vajradhara who bestowed Mahamudra teachings on the bodhisattva Lodro Rinchen Ratnamati, which teachings then come down to Tilopa and Naropa. In the case of the great masters who received Mahamudra lineage transmissions directly from the Buddha Vajradhara, those transmissions happened a long time after Prince Siddhartha's paranirvana. The physical Buddha, the historical Buddha Shakyamuni, Prince Siddhartha, was at the time no longer in physical Prince Siddhartha form. What happened was that first these great masters received the teachings of the Buddha and the Buddha's disciples through " distance lineages," and they practiced them. Through their practice they attained realization. As part of their realization the Buddha manifested to them, but not as Prince Siddhartha, as Buddha Vajradhara. So,

Buddha, the sambhogakaya of the Buddha, and the nirmanakaya of the Buddha, which is Prince Siddhartha in our case. The Buddha Vajradhara means all in one – the ever present Buddha, the timeless Buddha.

Then the Buddha Vajradhara transmitted directly to certain great masters, but only as a result of the realization of the teachings they had already received from their masters, whose teachings started with the historical Buddha. In this way, the Mahamudra lineage and many Vajrayana Buddhist lineages actually have distance lineage as well as close lineage. – *Tai Situ Rinpoche*

29. The Hevajra, the Guhyasamaja and the Mahamaya teachings were the three major tantric teachings that Marpa received in India. These along with the Six Yogas of Naropa and the Mahamudra teachings are the major practices of the Kagyu lineage.

30. Marpa made Milarepa build two towers of stone. After Milarepa had finished each one, Marpa made him tear it down and put each rock back where it came from and start over. The third tower remains standing in Tibet.

31. The section on Marpa's third trip to India details the students pleadings with Marpa not to go to India and then has Marpa's reply in a song.

32. This is referring to the great shrine and stupa at Bodhgaya where Buddha Shakyamuni was enlightened.

33. There are different kinds of conduct that are appropriate to different levels of the Vajrayana practice. Traditionally most practitioners and beginning Vajrayana students engage in a type of conduct that is called the "conduct of total goodness." This is basically a conduct of peacefulness and gentleness, of being tamed and disciplined. But when someone is very close to Buddhahood, there is an ultimate kind of conduct that is called the "conduct of total victory over all directions." By employing this type of conduct, a person will act in many different ways –they will appear extremely happy, sometimes extremely sad, sometimes extremely majestic and sometimes extremely miserable.

There are two reasons for engaging in this latter kind of conduct. First the effect of this is that they can actually tame their students by means of these changes. Also because these advanced practitioners are at the point close to Buddhahood, if a student actually does lose confidence in them because of the strange behavior they see, the practitioner can always bring them back by performing a miracle. So this kind of behavior of acting crazy can only be employed by someone who is highly realized. The second reason for engaging in this behavior is for their own benefit. This behavior hones or sharpens their realization by testing to see if they have any attachment to how people react to them or whether, when they appear to be miserable, their mind loses sight of the confidence that people have in them, or whether they become upset when people don't treat them with respect and so forth. So they are testing their own realization when they are at the brink of Buddhahood to see if they have completely abandoned ego, and they are also using it as a means to tame their disciples – *Thrangu Rinpoche*

34. This refers to phowa practice. At the time of death, it is said that the mind must leave the body through the aperture at the top of the head if one wants a higher birth. If the mind leaves through any other orifice such as the eyes, the ears, the mouth, or the anus, one will be reborn in a lower birth.

35. One might wonder how Marpa could be a siddha and also be very sad at the death of his son. Marpa was certainly a siddha, but siddhas can display sadness and they can display illness. What happens when one experiences the truth of dharmata is that conventional reality does not disappear. Although a siddha can see through conventional appearances, these appearances are still very vivid and, from time to time, it is appropriate for a siddha to demonstrate sadness and happiness as well as displaying sickness and health. We also have to distinguish between Buddhahood in the sutra path and Buddhahood in the Vajrayana. Buddhahood in the sutra path is compared to the presence of a garuda within its egg. In this analogy the egg is the body of the practitioner during their lifetime and the garuda is their Buddhahood or realization. Full fruition of Buddhahood is reaped by the siddha when their mind and body separate at death. In the case of the Shakyamuni Buddha his body was the karmic ripening of three innumerable periods, or eons, of gathering the accumulations that led to enlightenment in his final lifetime. So his body possessed the thirty-two major and eighty minor marks of physical perfection and so forth.

However, in the case of someone who attains Buddhahood through the practice of the Vajrayana, the practitioner attains Buddhahood in a single lifetime through directly experiencing the nature of phenomena. But they experience that Buddhahood within the situation of having a karmically inherited body and a karmically inherited disposition or personality, which to some extent they retain until they die. That is why siddhas might become sad. – *Thrangu Rinpoche*

36. Unlike the West, vultures are considered very auspicious birds and are associated with good omens much like the eagle is in the United States.

37. A "command seal" is a restriction on the transmission of a teaching; a seal of secrecy upon a teaching. This term is used for instructions that are of the most special nature, only to be transmitted to those students worthy of receiving them in the sense that they are certain to devote themselves to the practice and transmission of these instructions to appropriate people in the next generation. So instructions bearing a command seal are instructions that are not given to just anyone who comes and requests them. Some instructions are given to anybody regardless of whether or not they have confidence in them, whether or not they will practice them. These are not like that.

38. The Eleventh Trungpa tulku, Chogyam Trungpa Rinpoche (1938-1987), was the major Kagyu Tibetan pioneer in America and the Western world. He established Vajradhatu and Shambhala centers.

39. So I have explained a little bit about the connection between the biography or *namtar* of Marpa and that of Trungpa Rinpoche. In this connection, (This was given at Gampo Abbey which was founded by Trungpa Rinpoche and Thrangu Rinpoche was made its abbot.) I would like to express my appreciation to all of you for your great care in the maintenance of the archives, the tapes, videotapes, photographs, transcripts, the published books and texts, and so forth. If you ask, "Is it enough to take care of the texts and so forth that you have received at this point?" The answer is, "No." because that's just the first step. After the first step, then you have to take the second step, which is that these teachings that are contained in the archives must be properly propagated. Those that should be published must be published, and those that should be made available should be made available in the appropriate manner. The importance of Trungpa Rinpoche's writings and talks and so forth cannot be overemphasized. In this context, the following little story is pertinent.

In the early part of the twentieth century, there was a great scholar and teacher from Amdo named Gendun Chophel. Towards the end of his life, when he realized he was dying, he said to his students (by the way, Gendun Chophel smoked): "I wrote some things down on cigarette packages. Don't lose them."

However, if you ask, "Is just making the teachings available enough?" the answer again is "no." After the second step, you have to take the third which, in this case, is to make use of these teachings by studying them and training in the study of them as intensively as possible. Having taken those steps though is still not enough because you have to practice them and actually implement the meaning of the teachings in your life. And that still is not enough, because finally you have to train yourself to the point where you can teach them to future generations. In order to do this, you should develop courage and strength of mind so that you can aspire to the goal that Trungpa Rinpoche's teachings will remain undiminished until samsara is totally emptied. You could also reflect on the fact that this responsibility of maintaining and propagating his teachings does not rest with just one or two people. It's a responsibility that rests with all of you and if you view this as service to your root guru, it is that; if you view it as your practice, it is that. It's also the best possible inheritance you could leave to your children and your other descendants. — *Thrangu Rinpoche*

Glossary of Terms

Abhisheka. (Tib. *wang*) Empowerment. The conferring of power or authorization to practice the Vajrayana teachings, the indispensable entrance door to tantric practice. One should also receive the practice instruction (Tib. *tri*) and the textual reading (Tib. *lung*).

Aggregates, five. (Skt. *skandha*, Tib. *phung po nga*) Literally, "heaps." These are the five basic transformations that perceptions undergo when an object is perceived. First is form, which includes all sounds, smells, etc., everything that is not thought. The second and third are sensations (pleasant and unpleasant, etc.) and their identification. Fourth are mental events, which actually include the second and third aggregates. The fifth is ordinary consciousness, such as the sensory and mental consciousnesses.

Anuttarayoga tantra. (Tib. *nal jor la na me pay ju*) There are four levels of the Vajrayana and Anuttarayoga tantra is the highest of these. It contains the Guhyasamaja, the Chakrasamvara, the Hevajra and the Kalachakra tantras.

Atisha. (982-1055 C.E.) A Buddhist scholar at Nalanda University in India who came to Tibet at the invitation of the King to overcome the damage done by Langdarma. He helped found the Kadampa tradition.

Avalokiteshvara. (Tib. *Chenrezig*) The bodhisattva embodying the compassion of all the Buddhas. Depicted holding the wish-fulfilling gem between folded hands. One of the eight main bodhisattvas. The mantra associated with this bodhisattva is known as the king of mantras, OM MANI PEME HUNG.

Bardo. (Tib.) The intermediate state between the end of one life and rebirth into another. Bardo can also be divided into six different levels; the bardo of birth, dreams, meditation, the moment before death, the bardo of dharmata and the bardo of becoming.

Bindu. (Tib. *tigle)* Vital essence drops or spheres of psychic energy that are often visualized in Vajrayana practices.

Blessings. (Tib. *chin lap*) The process by which one individual introduces some of their accumulated merit into another's "stream of being." The ability to bestow blessing depends on the donor's degree of spiritual attainment and on the recipient's faith. The donor is usually the root-guru, whose blessing is said to contain that of all the sources of refuge combined. Although future experiences are largely shaped by present actions, the root-guru's blessing can partially modify this. That is, it can create conditions favourable to the maturation of any religious predispositions our past actions may have generated, giving us the inspiration and energy we require to begin practising. In this way, unless our acts have been extremely unwholesome, the guru's blessing can help us overcome conflicting emotions and other obstacles. Thus the guru's blessing helps us realize the Buddha-potential we all possess.

Bodhichitta. (Tib. *chang chup chi sem*) Literally, the mind of enlightenment. There are two kinds of bodhichitta: absolute bodhichitta, which is completely awakened mind that sees the emptiness of phenomena, and relative bodhichitta which is the aspiration to practice the six paramitas and free all beings from the suffering of samsara. In regard to relative bodhichitta there is also two kinds: aspiration bodhichitta and perseverance bodhichitta.

Bodhisattva. (Tib. *chang chup sem pa*) "Heroic mind." *Bodhi* means blossomed or enlightened, and *sattva* means heroic mind. Literally, one who exhibits the mind of enlightenment. Also an individual who has committed him or herself to the Mahayana path of compassion and the practice of the six paramitas to achieve buddhahood to free all beings from samsara. These are the heart or mind disciples of the Buddha.

Bodhisattva levels. (Skt. *bhumi,* Tib. *sa*) The levels or stages a bodhisattva goes through to reach enlightenment. These consist of ten levels in the sutra tradition and thirteen in the tantra tradition.

Bodhisattva vow. The vow to attain Buddhahood for the sake of all beings.

Buddha. (Tib. *sang gye*) An individual who attains, or the attainment of, complete enlightenment, such as the historical Shakyamuni Buddha.

Buddha Shakyamuni. (Tib. *shakya tubpa*) The Shakyamuni Buddha, often called the Gautama Buddha, refers to the fourth Buddha of this age, who lived between 563 and 483 BCE.

Buddhafield. (Tib. *sang gye kyi zhing*) 1) One of the realms of the five Buddha families, either as sambhogakaya or nirmanakaya. 2) Pure personal experience.

Buddhahood. (Tib. *sang gyas*) The perfect and complete enlightenment of dwelling in neither samsara nor nirvana. Expression of the realization of perfect enlightenment, which characterizes a Buddha. The attainment of buddhahood is the birthright of all beings. According to the teachings of Buddha, every sentient being has, or better is already, buddha nature; thus buddhahood cannot be "attained." It is much more a matter of experiencing the primordial perfection and realizing it in everyday life.

Buddha-essence. (Tib. *de shegs nying po*) The essential nature of all sentient beings. The potential for enlightenment.

Central channel. (Tib. *tsa uma*) There are three major subtle channels in the body: the right, left, and central channel. These channels are not anatomical ones but conduits through which subtle energy flows. The central channel runs roughly along (or perhaps inside the spine).

Chakra. A complex systematic description of physical and psychological energy channels.

Chakrasamvara. (Tib. *korlo dompa*) A meditational deity which belongs to the Anuttarayoga tantra set of teachings. A main yidam or tantra of the New Schools.

Channels, winds and essences. Nadi, prana and bindu; the constituents of the vajra body. These channels are not anatomical structures, but more like meridians in acupuncture. There are thousands of channels, but the three main channels that carry the subtle energy are the right, left and central channel. The central channel runs roughly along the spinal column while the right and left are on the sides of the central channel.

According to the yogic teachings of the path of skilful means, realization is attained through synchronization of body and mind. This may be achieved through meditating on nadi (channels), prana (energy), and bindu (drops) — the psychic components in the illusory body. Prana is the energy, or "wind," moving through the nadis. As is said, "Mind consciousness rides the horse of prana on the pathways of the nadis. The bindu is mind's nourishment."

Because of dualistic thinking, prana enters the left and right channels. This divergence of energy in the illusory body corresponds to the mental activity that falsely distinguishes between subject and object and leads to karmically determined activity. Through yogic practice, the pranas can be brought into the central channel and therefore transformed into wisdom-prana. Then the mind can recognize its fundamental nature, realizing all dharmas as unborn.

This belongs to advanced practice and can only be learned through direct oral transmission from an accomplished guru. Once the meditator is well established in the experience of the fundamental nature of mind, they can meditate on it directly, dissolving the nadi, prana, and bindu visualization. Meditation using the concept of psychic channels is regarded as being the completion stage with signs, and the formless practice which contemplates the nature of mind directly is the completion stage without signs

Chöd. (Tib.) This is pronounced "chö" and literally means "to cut off" and refers to a practice that is designed to cut off all ego involvement and defilements. The *mo chod* (female chod) practice was founded by the famous female saint Machig Labdron (1031 to 1129 C. E.).

Clarity. (Tib. *selwa*) Also translated as luminosity. The nature of mind is that it is empty of inherent existence, but the mind is not just voidness or completely empty because it has this clarity which is awareness or the knowing of mind. So clarity is a characteristic of emptiness (*shunyata*) of mind.

Completion stage. (Tib. *dzo rim*) In the Vajrayana there are two stages of meditation: the creation/development stage and the completion stage. Completion stage with marks is the six doctrines. Completion stage without marks is the practice of essence Mahamudra, resting in the unfabricated nature of mind.

Consciousnesses, sensory. These are the five sensory consciousnesses of sight, hearing, smell, taste, touch, and body sensation.

Consciousnesses, eight (Skt. *vijñana*, Tib. *nam she tsog gye*) These are the five sensory consciousnesses of sight, hearing, smell, taste, touch, and body sensation. Sixth is mental consciousness, seventh is afflicted consciousness, and eighth is ground consciousness.

Consciousnesses, six. The five sensory consciousnesses and the mental consciousness.

Creation stage. (Skt. *utpattikrama*, Tib. *che rim*) In the Vajrayana there are two stages of meditation: the development and the completion stage. The creation stage is a method of tantric meditation that involves the visualization and contemplation of deities for the purpose of purifying habitual tendencies and realizing the purity of all phenomena. In this stage visualization of the deity is established and maintained.

Daka. (Tib. *khandro*) A male counterpart to a dakini.

Dakini. (Tib. *khandroma*) A yogini who has attained high realizations of the fully enlightened mind. She may be a human being who has achieved such attainments or a non-human manifestation of the enlightened mind of a meditational deity. A female aspect of the protectors. It is feminine energy which has inner, outer and secret meanings.

Dharma. (Tib. *chö*) This has two main meanings: first, any truth, such as that the sky is blue; and secondly, the teachings of the Buddha (also called "Buddha-dharma").

Dharmachakra. Sanskrit for "Wheel of Dharma." The three vehicles of Buddhist practice; Hinayana, Mahayana and Vajrayana. When referring to the thirty-two marks of a Buddha it is the design of an eight-spoked wheel.

Dharma protector. (Skt. *dharmapala,* Tib. *cho kyong)* A Buddha, bodhisattva or powerful but ordinary being whose job is to remove all interferences and bestow all necessary conditions for the practice of pure dharma.

Dharmadhatu. (Tib. *chö ying*) The all-encompassing space, unoriginated and without beginning, out of which all phenomena arises. The Sanskrit means "the essence of phenomena" and the Tibetan means "the expanse of phenomena," but it usually refers to the emptiness that is the essence of phenomena.

Dharmakaya. (Tib. *chö ku*) One of the three bodies of buddhahood. It is enlightenment itself, that is, wisdom beyond any point of reference. (see *kayas, three.)*

Dharmaru. (Tib.) Ritual object used in Vajrayana practice.

Dharmata. (Tib. *chö nyi*) Dharmata is often translated as "suchness" or "the true nature of things" or "things as they are." It is phenomena as it really is or as seen by a completely enlightened being without any distortion or obscuration, so one can say it is "reality." The nature of phenomena and mind.

Disturbing emotions. (Skt. *klesha,* Tib. *nyön mong*) Also called the "afflictive emotions," these are the emotional afflictions or obscurations (in contrast to intellectual obscurations) that disturb the clarity of perception. These are also translated as "poisons." They include any emotion that disturbs or distorts consciousness. The main kleshas are desire, anger and ignorance.

Doha. (Tib. *gur*) A spiritual song spontaneously composed by a Vajrayana practitioner. It usually has nine syllables per line.

Dream practice (Tib. *mi lam*) An advanced Vajrayana practice using the dream state. This is one of the Six Yogas of Naropa (See *Six Yogas of Naropa).*

Eight consciousnesses. The all-ground consciousness, mind-consciousness, afflicted consciousness, and the five sense-consciousnesses. The Hinayana sutras generally discuss mind in terms of six consciousnesses, namely, the five sensory consciousnesses and the sixth mental consciousness. The Mahayana Cittamatra school (Mind-only) school talks about the eight consciousness in which the first six are the same but has the seventh and eighth consciousnesses added. In the Hinayana tradition the functions of the seventh and eighth consciousnesses are subsumed in the sixth mental consciousness.

Eight fold noble path. Right view, right thought, right speech, right action, right livelihood, right effort, right mindfulness and right concentration.

Eight freedoms & ten opportunities. (*Tal jor*) *Tal* is often translated as "freedom" and *jor* as "endowments," "qualities," "resources," and "opportunities" which constitute a precious human birth to practice dharma. The eight freedoms are traditionally enumerated as freedom from birth as a hell being, a hungry ghost, an animal, a barbarian, a long-lived god, a heretic, a mentally handicapped person, or living in a dark age (here meaning when no Buddha has come, in other contexts, according to the teachings on five degenerations we are living in a dark age). Of the ten conjunctions or resources, the five personal conjunctions are having a human body, being born in a land to which the dharma has spread, having all of one's senses intact, not reverting to evil ways, and having confidence in the three jewels. (Having one's senses impaired to the extent that one's mind could not function properly in the study and practice of dharma would constitute the loss of one's precious human birth.) The five conjunctions that come by way of others are that a Buddha has been born in this age, that the Buddha taught the dharma, that the dharma still exists, that there are still followers who have realized the meaning and essence of the teachings of the dharma, and there are benevolent sponsors.

Eight worldly concerns. (Tib. *jik ten chö gysh*) These keep one from the path; they are attachment to gain, attachment to pleasure, attachment to praise, attachment to fame, aversion to loss, aversion to pain, aversion to blame and aversion to a bad reputation.

Emptiness. (Tib. *tong pa nyi* Skt. *shunyata*) A central theme in Buddhism. It should not lead one to views of nihilism or the like, but is a term indicating the lack of any truly existing independent nature of any and all phenomena. Positively stated, phenomena do exist, but as mere appearances, interdependent manifestations of mind with no limitation. It is not that it is just your mind, as mind is also free of any true existence. This frees one from a solipsist view. This is interpreted differently by the individual schools.

Empowerment. (Tib. *wang* Skt. *abhiseka*) The conferring of power or authorization to practice the Vajrayana teachings, the indispensable entrance door to tantric practice. To do a Vajrayana practice one must receive the empowerment from a qualified lama. One should also receive the practice instruction (Tib. *tri*) and the textual reading (Tib. *lung*).

Enlightenment. (Skt. *bodhi* Tib. *jang chub*) According to the Buddhadharma, theistic and mystical experiences of all kinds still fall within samsara, as long as they confirm the experiencer or solidify the experience, even in the most subtle way. Buddhist norms of experience are: universal impermanence, existence as suffering, selflessness, and peace as absence of struggle to attain or maintain anything.

The Hinayana tradition defines enlightenment as the cessation of ignorance and of conflicting emotions, and therefore freedom from the compulsive rebirth in samsara. Its degrees of attainment were enumerated as four levels: stream enterer, once returner, non-returner and arhat.

According to the Mahayana tradition, Hinayana nirvana is a way station, like an illusory city in the desert created by the Buddha to encourage travellers. Enlightenment requires not only cessation of ignorance but also compassion and skilful means to work with the bewilderment of all sentient beings. The arhat does not attain complete enlightenment because of their undeveloped compassion.

According to the Vajrayana tradition, Hinayana and Mahayana attainment are necessary, but they contain dogma. It is necessary for the yogin to develop complete partnership with the phenomenal world and to experience a more penetrating unmasking of the root of ego. In presenting the final fruition, the Vajrayana teaches either four or six yanas.

The term nirvana can have the utmost positive sense when referring to enlightenment; or it can have a limiting or pejorative sense when referring to a limited goal of cessation.

Eternalism. (Tib. *rtag lta*) The belief that there is a permanent and causeless creator of everything; in particular, that one's identity or consciousness has a concrete essence which is independent, everlasting and singular.

Experience and realization. (Tib. *nyam togs*) An expression used for insight and progress on the path. "Experience" refers to temporary meditation experiences and "realization" to unchanging understanding of the nature of things.

Father tantra. (Tib. *pha gyu*) There are three kinds of tantras. The *father tantra* is concerned with transforming aggression, the *mother tantra* with transforming passion, and the *non-dual tantra* with transforming ignorance,

Five Buddha families. (Tib. *rig nga*) These are the Buddha, Vajra, Ratna, Padma and Karma families.

Five male Buddhas. Vairochana, Akshobhya, Ratnasambhava, Amitabha and Amoghasiddhi

Five female Buddhas. Dhatvishvari, Mamaki, Locana, Pandaravasini and Samayatara.

Five dhyani Buddhas. Vairochana, Akshobhya, Ratnasambhava, Amitabha and Amoghasiddhi. They are the pure aspects of the five elements and five emotions.

Five degeneration's. 1) the times, meaning the outer events of the world such as wars and social unrest are becoming worse, 2) of beings, meaning their mind-streams are becoming coarser, 3) length of life is becoming shorter, 4) increase in the emotional afflictions of beings, causing instability in their minds, 5) and degeneration of view, meaning people's understanding of reality is growing further from the truth. Based on these five degenerations we are now living in a dark age.

Five paths. (Tib. *lam nga*) According to the sutras there are five paths; the path of accumulation, the path of integration/junction, the path of seeing/insight, (attainment of the first bodhisattva level), the path of meditation, and the path of no more learning (buddhahood). The five paths cover the entire process from beginning dharma practice to complete enlightenment.

Five poisons. (Tib. *ldug nga*) Temporary mental states that inhibit understanding: ignorance, pride, anger, desire, and jealousy. The three root poisons are ignorance, desire and anger.

Five wisdoms. The dharmadhatu wisdom, mirror-like wisdom, wisdom of equality, discriminating wisdom and all-accomplishing wisdom. They should not be understood as separate entities but rather as different functions of one's enlightened essence.

Four empowerments. (Tib. *wang shi*) The empowerments of vase, secret, wisdom-knowledge and precious word.

Four extremes (Tib. *tha shi*) Existence, non-existence, both and neither.

Four reminders. The four ordinary foundations: the difficulty in obtaining the precious human body; impermanence and death; karma, cause and effect; the shortcomings of samsara. Reflection on these four reminders causes the mind to change and become directed toward the dharma.

Four seals. The four main principles of Buddhism: all compounded phenomena are impermanent, everything defiled (with ego-clinging) is suffering, all phenomena are empty and devoid of a self-entity, and nirvana is perfect peace.

Four truths. The Buddha's first teachings. 1) All conditioned life is suffering. 2) All suffering is caused by ignorance. 3) Suffering can cease. 4) The eight-fold path leads to the end of suffering: right understanding, thought, speech, action, livelihood, effort, mindfulness and meditation.

Four Yogas of Mahamudra. (Tib. *phyag chen gyi nal byor zhi*) Four stages in Mahamudra practice: one-pointedness, simplicity, one taste and nonmeditation.

Graded path. This refers to being guided through the path to enlightenment through the three principle paths, 1) renunciation, 2) enlightened motive of bodhicitta, 3) and a correct understanding of emptiness (wisdom).

Gampopa. (1079-1153 C.E.) One of the main lineage holders of the Kagyu lineage in Tibet. A student of Milarepa he established the first Kagyu monastic monastery and is known also for writing the *Jewel Ornament of Liberation.*

Ganacakra (Tib. *tog kyi kor lo*) This is a ritual feast offering which is part of a spiritual practice.

Garuda (Tib. *khyung*) A mythical bird that hatches fully grown.

Guru. (Tib. *lama*) A teacher in the Tibetan tradition who has reached realization.

Guru yoga. (Tib. *lamay naljor*) A practice of devotion to the guru culminating in receiving his blessing and blending indivisibly with his mind. Also refers to the fourth practice of the preliminary practices of ngöndro.

Guhyasamaja tantra. (Tib. *sang pa dus pa*) Literally, "Assembly of Secrets." One of the major tantras and yidams of the New School. This is the "father tantra" of the Anuttarayoga, which is the highest of the four tantras. Guhyasamaja is the central deity of the vajra family.

Hearing lineage. (Tib. *nyan gyu*) A lineage of instruction passed orally from teacher to disciple. Teachings of a hearing lineage are usually very secret, since they can only be received by direct, personal communication with the guru. "Hearing lineage" is also a common epithet for the Kagyu lineage.

Heruka. (Tib. *trak thung*) A wrathful male deity.

Hevajra. (Tib. *kye dorje*) This is the "mother tantra" of the Anuttarayoga tantra, which is the highest of the four yogas. "He" is said to be an exclamation of joy. Hevajra transforms sense pleasures into joy through the realization of the identity of form and emptiness. He is depicted in two, four, six, twelve, and sixteen-armed forms, dancing in union with his consort, usually Nairatmya.

Hevajra tantra. (Tib. *kye dorje*) This is the "mother tantra" of the Anuttarayoga tantra, which is the highest of the four yogas.

Higher realms. The three higher realms are birth as a human, demi-god and god.

Hinayana. (Tib. *tek pa chung wa*) Literally, the "lesser vehicle." The first of the three *yanas,* or vehicles. The term refers to the first teachings of the Buddha, which emphasized the careful examination of mind and its confusion. It is the foundation of Buddha's teachings focusing mainly on the four truths and the twelve interdependent links. The fruit is liberation for oneself.

Idiot compassion. This is the desire to help others but it is not accompanied by sufficient wisdom, so that what one does may not really be beneficial. An example is teaching someone who is hungry to fish, yet the person receives negative karma for killing the fish.

Illusory body. (Tib. *gyu lu*) The transformation of a practitioner's very subtle energy body into a deathless miracle body of the deity during the completion stages. When this is purified it becomes the form body of the Buddha, one of the Six Yogas of Naropa. (see *Six Yogas of Naropa*)

Interdependent origination. The twelve links of causal connections which binds beings to samsaric existence and thus perpetuate suffering: ignorance, karmic formation, consciousness, name and form, the six sense bases, contact, sensation, craving, grasping, becoming, rebirth, old age, and death. These twelve links are like an uninterrupted vicious circle, a wheel that spins all sentient beings around and around through the realms of samsara.

Jnana. (Tib. *yeshe*) Enlightened wisdom that is beyond dualistic thought.

Jnanasattva. Jnana is awareness and *sattva* means mind.

Kadampa. (Tib.) One of the major schools in Tibet, it was founded by Atisha (993-1054 C.E.).

Kanjur. The preserved collection of the direct teaching of the Buddha.

Kagyu. (Tib.) *Ka* means oral and *gyu* means lineage; The lineage of oral transmission. One of the four major schools of Buddhism in Tibet. It was founded in Tibet by Marpa and is headed by His Holiness Karmapa. The other three are the Nyingma, the Sakya and the Gelugpa schools.

Kalachakra. A tantra and a Vajrayana system taught by Buddha Shakyamuni.

Kalpa (Tib. *kal pa,* Skt. *yuga*) An eon that lasts in the order of millions of years.

Karma. (Tib. *lay*) Literally "action." The unerring law of cause and effect, eg. Positive actions bring happiness and negative actions bring suffering. The actions of each sentient being are the causes that create the conditions for rebirth and the circumstances in that lifetime.

Karma Kagyu. (Tib.) One of the eight schools of the Kagyu lineage of Tibetan Buddhism which is headed by His Holiness Karmapa.

Karmapa. The name means Buddha activities. The Karmapas are the head of the Kagyu school of Buddhism and were the first to implement the tradition of incarnate lamas. Karmapas are thought to be an emanation of the bodhisattva Avalokiteshvara.

Karmic latencies or imprints. (Skt. *vasana,* Tib. *pakchak*) Every action and that a person does has an imprint which is stored in the eighth consciousness. These latencies express themselves later by leaving the eighth consciousness and entering the sixth consciousness upon being stimulated by external experience.

Kayas, three. (Tib. *ku sum*) There are three bodies of the Buddha: the nirmanakaya, sambhogakaya and dharmakaya. The dharmakaya, also called the "truth body," is the complete enlightenment or the complete wisdom of the Buddha that is unoriginated wisdom beyond form and manifests in the sambhogakaya and the nirmanakaya. The sambhogakaya, also called the "enjoyment body," manifests only to bodhisattvas. The nirmanakaya, also called the "emanation body," manifests in the world and in this context manifests as the Shakyamuni Buddha. The fourth kaya is the svabhavakakaya, the "essence body" which is the unity of the other three.

Key instructions — a text's key instruction rests upon establishing the line of reasoning in a teaching. Seeing this line of reasoning, we can distinguish between the form and the content of the teachings. What key instructions do are wake a person up to the true nature of the experience that the teachings generate, such as the dissolving of the objective form of the experience, which can be seen as it truly is, appreciated as having no independent reality and hence no power, as would be the case if it existed independently. The key instruction that, if acted upon, generates a liberating personality transformation, is repeated at each level of the teachings.

King Indrabhutii. An Indian king during the time of the Buddha who become an accomplished master. He symbolizes the person of the highest calibre who can use sense pleasures as the path of practice.

Klesha. (Tib. *nyön mong*) Also called the "afflictive emotions," these are the emotional afflictions or obscurations (in contrast to intellectual obscurations) that disturb the clarity of perception. These are also translated as "poisons." They include any emotion that disturbs or distorts consciousness. The three main kleshas are desire, anger and ignorance. The five kleshas are the three above plus pride and envy/jealousy.

Kriya tantra. (Tib. *ja way gyu*) One of the four tantras which emphasizes personal purity.

Kukkuripa. (Tib. *Shiwa Sangpo*) The noted holders of the Yamantaka lineage of the Madhyamaka School of Indian Buddhist thought include siddha Saraha, siddha Lawapa, siddha Virupa and siddha Kukuri (*aka* Kukuripa). Mahamudra arose from Madhyamaka thought, which, however, remains obscure, especially during the period when Buddhist thought was first introduced to Tibet. A famous thangka portrays Kukkuripa as a "wild yogi" at play among wild dogs.

Lama. (Skt. *guru*) *La* nobody above himself or herself in spiritual experience and *ma* expressing compassion like a mother. Thus the union of wisdom and compassion, feminine and masculine qualities. Lama is also a title given to a practitioner who has completed some extended training.

Liberation. (see *enlightenment*)

Lojong. Mind Training. The Mahayana meditation system of the early Kadampa school, brought to Tibet by Atisha.

Lotsawa. Sanskrit for "translator."

Lower realm. The three lower realms are birth as a hell being, hungry ghost and animal.

Luminosity. (Tib. *osel*) Literally "free from the darkness of unknowing and endowed with the ability to cognize." The two aspects are "empty luminosity," like a clear open sky; and "manifest luminosity," such as colored light images, and so forth. Luminosity is the uncompounded nature present throughout all of samsara and nirvana.

Madhyamaka. (Tib. *u ma*) The most influential of the four schools of Indian Buddhism founded by Nagarjuna in the second century C.E. The name comes from the Sanskrit word meaning "the Middle-way" meaning it is the middle way between eternalism and nihilism. The main postulate of this school is that all phenomena – both internal mental events and external physical objects – are empty of any true nature. The school uses extensive rational reasoning to establish the emptiness of phenomena. This school does, however, hold that phenomena do exist on the conventional or relative level of reality.

Mahakala. Dharmapala. A protector of the dharma and dharma practitioners.

Mahamaya tantra. (Tib. *gyu ma chen mo*) The mother tantra of the Anuttarayoga tantra, which is one of the four main tantras in Tibet.

Mahamudra. (Tib. *cha ja chen po*) Literally means "great seal" or "great symbol" meaning that all phenomena are sealed by the primordially perfect true nature. This form of meditation is traced back to Saraha (10th century) and was passed down in the Kagyu school through Marpa. This meditative transmission emphasizes perceiving mind directly rather than through rational analysis. It also refers to the experience of the practitioner where one attains the union of emptiness and luminosity and also perceives the non-duality of the phenomenal world and emptiness; also the name of Kagyupa lineage.

Mahapandita. (Tib. *pan di ta chen po*) *Maha* means great and *pandita* Buddhist scholar.

Mahasiddha. (Tib. *drup thop chen po)* A practitioner who has a great deal of realization. *Maha* means great and *siddha* refers to an accomplished practitioner. These were particularly vajrayana practitioners who lived in India between the eight and twelfth century and practiced tantra. The biography of some of the most famous is found in *The Eighty-four Mahasiddhas.*

Mahayana. (Tib. *tek pa chen po*) Literally, the "Great Vehicle." These are the teachings of the second turning of the wheel of dharma, which emphasize shunyata (see *shunyata*), compassion and universal buddha nature. The purpose of enlightenment is to liberate all sentient beings from suffering as well as oneself. Mahayana schools of philosophy appeared several hundred years after the Buddha's death, although the tradition is traced to a teaching he is said to have given at Rajgriha, or Vulture Peak Mountain.

Maitripa – was a guru of Marpa, the Tibetan forefather of the Kagyu lineage. Thus it is through Maitripa that Maitreya and Asanga's crucial work on Buddha nature, the Uttaratantrasastra (*Anuttara*), became widely followed in Tibet. It is said that he had been a student of Naropa when the latter was head of Nalanda monastic university. Maitripa also transmitted to Marpa the esoteric aspect of Buddha nature embodied in the Mahamudra teachings, which treat the topic of mind in great detail and provide a wide range of progressive, highly refined meditations. Maitripa was brought to enlightenment through Mahamudra under his guru Savari, who received the complete teachings of Mahamudra from Nagarjuna, who received them from Sahara, whom Marpa encountered in his dream state.

Mala. (Tib. *trengwa*) A rosary-like loop that usually has 108 beads.

Mandala. (Tib. *chil kor*) Literally "centre and surrounding" but has different contexts. A diagram used in various Vajrayana practices that usually has a central deity and four directions.

Manjushri. One of the eight bodhisattvas. He is the personification of transcendent knowledge.

Mantra. (Tib. *ngags*) The energy of sound. A power-laden syllable or series of syllables that manifests certain universal forces and aspects of the Buddhas, sometimes also the name of a buddha. Continuous repetition of mantras is practiced as a form of meditation in many Buddhist schools. In Tibetan Buddhism mantra is defined as a means of protecting the mind. In the transformation of body, speech and mind that is brought about by spiritual practice, mantra is associated with speech, and its task is the sublimation of the vibrations developed in the act of speaking. Recitation of mantras is always done in connection with detailed visualizations and certain bodily postures.

In the Tibetan tradition, the function of mantra is defined differently for the individual classes of the Tantras. In reciting for example, concentration on the sacred written form of the syllables is distinguished from concentration on their sound.

Mantra vehicle. Another term for the vajrayana.

Mara. (Tib. *du*) Difficulties encountered by the practitioner. The Tibetan word means heavy or thick. In Buddhism mara symbolizes the passions that overwhelm human beings as well as everything that hinders the arising of wholesome roots and progress on the path to enlightenment. There are four kinds: *skandha-mara*, which is incorrect view of self; *klesha-mara*, which is being overpowered by negative emotions; *matyu-mara*, which is death and interrupts spiritual practice; and *devaputra-mara*, which is becoming stuck in the bliss that comes from meditation.

Marpa. (1012-1097 C.E.) Marpa was known for being a Tibetan who made three trips to India and brought back many tantric texts, including the Six Yogas of Naropa, the Guhyasamaja, and the Chakrasamvara practices. His root teacher was Tilopa, the founder of the Kagyu lineage and the teacher of Naropa. Marpa initiated and founded the Kagyu lineage in Tibet.

Mental factors. (Tib. *sem yung*) Mental factors are contrasted to mind in that they are more long-term propensities of mind including eleven virtuous factors such as faith, detachment, and equanimity, and the six root defilements such as desire, anger, and pride, and the twenty secondary defilements such as resentment, dishonesty, harmfulness.

Milarepa. (1040-1123 C.E.) Milarepa was a student of Marpa who attained enlightenment in one lifetime. *Mila,* named by the deities and *repa* means white cotton. His student Gampopa established the (*Dagpo*) Kagyu lineage in Tibet.

Mind-only school. Also called Cittamatra school. This is one of the major schools in the mahayana tradition founded in the fourth century by Asanga that emphasized everything is mental events.

Mother tantra. (Tib. *ma gyu*) There are three kinds tantras: *the father tantra*, which is concerned with transforming aggression; the *mother tantra*, which is concerned with transforming passion and the non-dual tantra, which concerns transforming ignorance.

Mudra. (Tib. *chak gya*) In this book it is a "hand seal" or gesture that is performed in specific tantric rituals to symbolize certain aspects of the practice being done. Also can mean spiritual consort, or the "bodily form" of a deity.

Nadi. The channels in the vajra body through which the winds flow.

Naga. (Tib. *lu*) A water spirit which may take the form of a serpent. It is often the custodian of treasures either texts or actual material treasures under ground.

Nagarjuna. (Tib. *ludrup*) An Indian master of philosophy. Founder of the

Madhyamaka school and author of the *Mula-prajna* and other important works. (2nd - 3rd century)

Nalanda. The greatest Buddhist University from the fifth to the 10th century located near modern Rajgir which was the seat of the Mahayana teachings and had many great Buddhist scholars who studied there.

Naropa. (956-1040 C.E.) An Indian master best known for transmitting many Vajrayana teachings to Marpa who took these back to Tibet before the Moslem invasion of India.

Ngöndro. Tibetan for preliminary practice. One usually begins the vajrayana path by doing the four preliminary practices which involve about 111,000 refuge prayers and prostrations, 111,000 Vajrasattva mantras, 111,000 mandala offerings, and 111,000 guru yoga practices.

Nihilism. (Tib. *chad lta*) Literally, "the view of discontinuance." The extreme view of nothingness: no rebirth or karmic effects, and the non-existence of a mind after death.

Nirmanakaya. (Tib. *tulku*) There are three bodies of the Buddha and the nirmanakaya or "emanation body" manifests in the world and in this context manifests as the Shakyamuni Buddha. (see *kayas, three.*)

Nirvana. (Tib. *nyangde*) Literally, "extinguished." Individuals live in samsara and with spiritual practice can attain a state of enlightenment in which all false ideas and conflicting emotions have been extinguished. This is called nirvana. The nirvana of a Hinayana practitioner is freedom from cyclic existence, an arhat. The nirvana of a Mahayana practitioner is buddhahood, free from extremes of dwelling in either samsara or the perfect peace of an arhat.

Nondistraction. (Tib. *yengs med*) Not straying from the continuity of the practice.

Nonfabrication. (Tib. *zo med*) The important key point in meditation of Mahamudra and Dzogchen; that inate wakefulness is not created through intellectual effort.

Nonmeditation. (Tib. *gom med*) The state of not holding on to an object meditated upon nor a subject who meditates. Also refers to the fourth stage of Mahamudra in which nothing further needs to be meditated upon or cultivated.

Nonthought. (Tib. *mi tog*) A state in which conceptual thinking is absent.

Nyingma. (Tib.) The oldest school of Buddhism based on the teachings of Padmasambhava and others in the eighth and ninth centuries.

Obscurations. There are two categories of obscurations or defilements that cover one's buddha nature: the defilement of conflicting emotions (see *five poisons & afflictive obscurations*) and the defilement of latent tendencies or sometimes called the obscuration of dualistic perception, or the intellectual/cognitive obscurations (see *cognitive obscurations*). The first category prevents sentient beings from freeing themselves from samsara, while the second prevents them from gaining accurate knowledge and realising truth.

Occurrence. (Tib. *gyu ba*) The period when thoughts are arising in the mind. Compare with "stillness."

One-pointedness. (Tib. *Tse cig*) The first stage in the practice of Mahamudra.

One taste, (Tib. *ro cig*) The third stage in the practice of Mahamudra.

Oral instructions. (Tib. *man ngag, dams ngag*) As opposed to the scholastic traditions, the oral instructions of the Practice lineages are concise and pithy so they can always be kept in ind; they are practical and to the point so they are effective means to deal directly with the practice.

Pandita. A great scholar.

Paramita. "Transcendental" or "Perfection." Pure actions free from dualistic concepts that liberate sentient beings from samsara. The six paramitas are: diligence, patience, morality, generosity, contemplation, and transcendental knowledge or insight.

Path of Liberation. (Tib. *drol lam*) The path of Mahamudra practice.

Path of Means. (Tib. *thab lam*) Refers to the Six Yogas of Naropa as well as to the stages of creation and completion with attributes.

Partial compassion. The desire to feel sorry for and want to help others, but only if they are of a certain gender, race, ethnic group, social status, etc.

Paranirvana. After the Buddha Shakyamuni passed from this realm: Buddhas are not said to have died, since they have reached the stage of deathlessness, or deathless awareness.

Phowa. (Tib.) There are different kinds of phowa practice. The highest result of *dharmakaya phowa* and *sambhogakaya phowa* is full enlightenment. In this text, reference has primarily been to *nirmanakaya phowa*, called "the phowa that one practices" and to *Kacho Phowa*, an advanced tantric practice of dream yoga and clear light yoga concerned with the ejection of consciousness at death to a favourable realm or rebirth.

Pointing-out instructions. (Tib. *ngo sprod kyi gdampa*) The direct introduction to the nature of mind.

Prana. Life supporting energy. The "winds" or energy-currents of the vajra body.

Prajna. (Tib. *she rab*) In Sanskrit it means "perfect knowledge" and can mean wisdom, understanding or discrimination. Usually it means the wisdom of seeing things from a high (e.g. non-dualistic) point of view.

Prajnaparamita. (Tib. *she rab chi parol tu chinpa)* Transcendent perfect knowledge.

The Tibetan literally means, "gone to the other side" or "gone beyond" as expressed in the prajnaparamita mantra, "Om gate gate paragate parasamgate bodhi svaha." The realization of emptiness in the Prajnaparamita Hridaya or Heart Sutra made possible by the extraordinarily profound dharma of the birth of Shakyamuni Buddha in the world and the practices that came from it, such as the Vajrayana tantras, which make use of visualization and the control of subtle physical energies.

Prajnaparamita sutras. Used to refer to a collection of about 40 Mahayana sutras that all deal with the realization of prajna.

Pratyekabuddha. "Solitary Awakened One." These are the body disciples of the Buddha. One who has attained awakening for himself, and on his own, with no teacher in that life. Generally placed on a level between arhat and Buddha. It is the fruition of the second level of the Hinayana path through contemplation on the twelve interdependent links in reverse order.

Provisional meaning. The teachings of the Buddha which have been simplified or modified to the capabilities of the audience. This contrasts with the definitive meaning.

Rangtong school. The Madhyamaka or Middle-way is divided into two major schools; Rangtong (empty of self) and Shentong (empty of other). Rangtong is from the second turning of the wheel of dharma and teaches reality is empty of self and beyond concepts.

Recognition. (Tib. *ngo shes, ngo phrod*) In this context it means "recognizing the nature of mind."

Relative truth. (Tib. *kunsop*) There are two truths: relative and absolute or ultimate truth. Relative truth is the perception of an ordinary (unenlightened) being who sees the world with all his or her projections based on the false belief in "I" and "other."

Root lama. (Tib. *tsa way lama*) A practitioner of Vajrayana can have several types of root guru: the vajra master who confers empowerment, who bestows reading transmission, or who explains the meaning of the tantras. The ultimate root guru is the master who gives the "pointing out instructions" so that one recognizes the nature of mind.

Rupakaya. (Tib. *zuk kyi ku*) The form bodies that encompass the sambhogakaya and the nirmanakaya.

Sacred outlook. (Tib. *dag snang*) Awareness and compassion lead the practitioner to experience emptiness (*shunyata*). From that comes luminosity manifesting as the purity and sacredness of the phenomenal world. Since the sacredness comes out of the experience of emptiness, the absence of preconceptions, it is neither a religious nor a secular vision: that is, spiritual and secular vision could meet. Moreover, sacred outlook is not conferred by any god. Seen clearly, the world is self-existingly sacred.

Sadhana. (Tib. *drup tap*) Tantric liturgy and procedure for practice, usually emphasizing the generation stage.

Samadhi. (Tib. *tin ne zin*) A state of meditation that is non-dualistic. There is an absence of discrimination between self and other. Also called meditative absorption or one-pointed meditation; this is the highest form of meditation.

Samaya. (Tib. *dam sig*) The vows or commitments made in the Vajrayana to a teacher or to a practice. Many details exist but essentially it consists of outwardly, maintaining a harmonious relationship with the vajra master and one's dharma friends and inwardly, not straying from the continuity of the practice.

Sambhogakaya. (Tib. *long chö dzok ku*) There are three bodies of the Buddha and the sambhogakaya, also called the "enjoyment body," is a realm of the dharmakaya that only manifests to bodhisattvas (see *kayas, three*).

Samsara. (Tib. *kor wa*) "Cyclic existence." The conditioned existence of ordinary life in which suffering occurs because one still possesses attachment, aggression and ignorance. It is contrasted to nirvana. Through the force of karma motivated by ignorance, desire and anger one is forced to take on the impure aggregates and circle the wheel of existence until liberation.

Sangha. (Tib. *gen dun*) "Virtuous One." *Sang* means intention or motivation and *gha* means virtuous. One with virtuous motivation. One of the three jewels. Generally refers to the followers of Buddhism, and more specifically to the community of monks and nuns. The exalted sangha is those who have attained a certain level of realization of the Buddha's teachings.

Saraha. (*circa* 9th century) One of the eighty-four mahasiddhas of India who was known for his spiritual songs about Mahamudra.

Secret mantra. (Tib. *sang ngak*) A name for the vajrayana.

Selflessness. (Tib. *dag me*) Also called egolessness. In two of the hinayana schools (Vaibhashika and Sautrantika) this referred exclusively to the fact that "a person" is not a real permanent self, but rather just a collection of thoughts and feelings. In two of the mahayana schools (Cittamatra and Madhyamaka) this was extended to mean there was no inherent existence to outside phenomena as well.

Sending and taking practice. (Tib. *tong len*) A meditation practice promulgated by Atisha in which the practitioner takes on the negative conditions of others and gives out all that is positive.

Sentient beings. With consciousness, an animated being as opposed to an inanimate object. All beings with consciousness or mind who have not attained the liberation of buddhahood. This includes those individuals caught in the sufferings of samsara as well as those who have attained the levels of a bodhisattva.

Seven dharmas of Vairochana. These are the main positions of posture for meditation: (1) Straighten the upper body and the spinal column, (2) Look slightly downward into space straight across from the tip of the nose while keeping the chin and neck straight, (3) Straighten the shoulder blades in the manner of a vulture flexing its wings, (4) Keep the lips touching gently, (5) Let the tip of the tongue touch the upper palate, (6) Form the legs into either the lotus (Skt. *padmasana*) or the diamond (Skt. *vajrasana*) posture, and (7) Keep the back of the right hand flat on the left open palm with the inside of the tips of the thumbs gently touching.

Shamatha. (Tib.) See tranquillity meditation.

Shastra. (Tib. *tan chö*) The Buddhist teachings are divided into words of the Buddha (the *sutras*) and the commentaries of others on his works the (*shastras*).

Shentong school. The Madhyamaka or Middle-way is divided into two major schools; Rangtong (empty of self) and Shentong (empty of other). Shentong is from the third turning of the wheel of dharma and explains ultimate reality is emptiness and luminosity inseparable.

Shravaka. "Hearer" corresponds to the level of arhat, those that seek and attain liberation for oneself through listening to the Buddhas teaching and gaining insight into selflessness and the four truths. These are the Buddhas speech disciples.

Siddha. (Tib. *drup top*) An accomplished Buddhist practitioner.

Siddhi. (Tib. *ngodrup*) "Accomplishment." The spiritual accomplishments of accomplished practitioners. Usually refers to the "supreme siddhi" of complete enlightenment, but can also mean the "common siddhis," eight mundane accomplishments.

Simplicity. (Tib. *spros ral*) 1) The absence of creating mental constructs or conceptual formations about the nature of things. 2) The second stage in the practice of Mahamudra.

Six consciousnesses. The five sensory consciousnesses and the mental consciousness.

Six realms. The realms of the six classes of beings: gods, demigods, humans, animals, hungry ghosts and hell beings.

Six Yogas of Naropa. (Tib. *naro chödruk*) These six special yogic practices were transmitted from Naropa to Marpa and consist of the subtle heat practice, the illusory body practice, the dream yoga practice, the luminosity practice, the ejection of consciousness practice and the bardo practice.

Skandha. (Tib. *pung pa*) Literally "heaps." These are the five basic transformations that perceptions undergo when an object is perceived: form, feeling, perception, formation and consciousness. First is form, which includes all sounds, smells, etc.; everything we usually think of as outside the mind. The second and third are sensations (pleasant and unpleasant, etc.) and their identification. Fourth is mental events, which include the second and third aggregates. The fifth is ordinary consciousness, such as the sensory and mental consciousnesses.

Skilful means. (Skt. *upaya*, Tib. *thabs*) Generally, this conveys the sense that enlightened beings teach the dharma skilfully, taking into consideration the various needs, abilities, and shortcomings of their students. Upaya is an expression of compassion. In the bodhisattva's discipline, it corresponds to the first five paramitas and to relative bodhicitta. By prajna alone, without upaya, the bodhisattva is fettered to a quietistic nirvana. By upaya without prajna, one remains bound to samsara. Therefore the practitioner must unify them.

In Vajrayana, upaya arises from shunyata. It is joined with prajna and represents the male, form aspect of the union of form and emptiness.

Spiritual song. (Skt. *doha*, Tib. *gur*) A religious song spontaneously composed by a Vajrayana practitioner. It usually has nine syllables per line.

Stillness. (Tib. *gnas pa*) Absence of thought activity and disturbing emotions, but with subtle fixation on this stillness.

Stupa. (Tib. *chorten*) Objects of offering, or objects for accumulating. A stupa is a monument symbolic of the dharmakaya and contains the relics of Buddhas or other enlightened beings. These, like your Guru, are focal points for veneration and our path to buddhahood. Any disrespectful act toward them is disrespect for enlightenment itself.

Subtle channels. (Skt. *nadi*, Tib. *tsa*) These refer to the subtle channels which are not anatomical ones but ones in which psychic energies or "winds" (Skt. *prana*, Tib. *lung*) travel.

Sugata. An epithet for the Buddha.

Sugatagarbha. The buddha nature.

Supreme siddhi. Another word for enlightenment.

Sutra. (Tib. *do*) Literally "Junction." The combination of the Hinayana and Mahayana, or the combination of wisdom and compassion. Texts in the Buddhist cannon attributed to the Buddha. They are viewed as his recorded words, although they were not actually written down until many years after his *paranirvana*. They are usually in the form of dialogues between the Buddha and his disciples. These are often contrasted with the tantras which are the Buddha's Vajrayana teachings and the shastras which are commentaries on the words of the Buddha.

Sutra Mahamudra. (Tib. *mdo'i phyag chen*) The Mahamudra system based on the Prajnaparamita scriptures and emphasizing Shamatha and Vipashyana and the progressive journey through the five paths and ten bhumis.

Sutrayana. The sutra approach to achieving enlightenment which includes the Hinayana and the Mahayana.

Svabhavakakaya. (Tib. *ngo bo nyid kyi sku*) The "essence body." Sometimes counted as the fourth kaya, the unity of the first three.

Tantra. (Tib. *gyu*.) Literally, tantra means "continuity," and in Buddhism it refers to two specific things: the texts (resultant texts, or those that take the result as the path) that describe the practices leading from ignorance to enlightenment, including commentaries by tantric masters; and the way to enlightenment itself, encompassing the ground, path, and fruition. One can divide Buddhism into the sutra tradition and the tantra tradition. The sutra tradition primarily involves the academic study of the Mahayana sutras and the tantric path primarily involves practicing the Vajrayana practices. The tantras are primarily the texts of the Vajrayana practices.

Tantra Mahamudra (Tib. *sngags kyi phyag chen*) The same as mantra Mahamudra. The Mahamudra practice connected to the six dharmas of Naropa.

Tathagatagarbha. The same as Buddhanature. The inherently present potential for enlightenment in all sentient beings.

Ten non-virtuous actions. Killing, stealing, sexual misconduct, lying, slander, abusive words, idle gossip, covetousness, ill-will, and wrong views. Acts are non-virtuous or unwholesome when they result in undesirable karmic effects. Thus, this list of ten unwholesome acts occurs generally in discussions of the functioning of karma. The first three are actions of body, the next four of speech, and the last three of mind. The ten virtuous actions are the opposites of the above ten non-virtuous actions.

Ten stages. The stages or bodhisattva levels in the Mahayana path which are: 1) The Joyous One with an emphasis on generosity, 2) The Stainless One with an emphasis on discipline, 3) The Illuminating One with an emphasis on patience, 4) The Flaming One with an emphasis on exertion, 5) The One Difficult to Conquer with an emphasis on samadhi, 6) The Manifest One with an emphasis on wisdom, 7) The Far Going One with an emphasis on skilful activity, 8) The Unshakeable One with an emphasis on future, 9) The One of Good Discrimination with an emphasis on efficacy, 10) Cloud of Dharma with an emphasis on accomplishing enlightenment. In the tantric (Vajrayana) literature there are three more stages of manifesting enlightenment, making thirteen in total.

Tenjur. Commentary on the Kanjur; also tantras of meditation, healing, scientific and technical instructions etc.

Thangka. Religious cloth scroll painting, depicting various aspects of enlightenment.

Three jewels. (Tib. *kön chok sum*) Literally "three precious ones." The three essential components of Buddhism: Buddha, dharma, sangha, i.e., the Awakened One, the truth expounded by him, and the followers living in accordance with this truth. Firm faith in the three precious ones is the stage of "stream entry." The three precious ones are objects of veneration and are considered "places of refuge." The Buddhist takes refuge by pronouncing the threefold refuge formula, thus acknowledging formally to be a Buddhist.

Three realms. These are three categories of samsara. The desire realm includes existences where beings are reborn with solid bodies due to their karma ranging from the deva paradises to the hell realms. The form realm is where beings are reborn due to the power of meditation; and their bodies are of subtle form in this realm. These are the meditation paradises. The formless realm is where beings due to their meditation (samadhi), have entered a state of meditation after death and the processes of thought and perception have ceased.

Three roots. Guru, yidam and dakini. Guru is the root of blessings, yidam of accomplishment and dakini of activity.

Three sufferings. These are the suffering of suffering, the suffering of change, and pervasive suffering (meaning the inherent suffering in all of samsara).

Three vehicles. Hinayana, Mahayana and Vajrayana.

Tilopa. (928-1009 C.E.) One of the eighty-four mahasiddhas who became the guru of Naropa who transmitted his teachings to the Kagyu lineage in Tibet.

Torma. (Tib.) A sculpture made out of tsampa and moulded butter, used as a shrine offering, a feast offering substance, or as a representation of deities. There are traditional designs for each of the many types of torma.

Tranquillity meditation. (Tib. *Shinay*, Skt. *Shamatha*) One of the two main types of meditation, calm abiding, the meditative practice of calming the mind in order to rest free from the disturbance of thought activity; the other is insight or Vipashyana.

Tulku. (Tib. Skt. *nirmanakaya*) The Tibetan means "Multiple body." It is the term used for describing the emanation body of an enlightened being or bodhisattva. The syllable *tul* has both direct and indirect meanings. The direct meaning is "multiple" and the indirect meaning, "manifestation," which refers to the sending out of compassion. It is the illusory emanation of the dharmakaya as a nirmanakaya form. *Ku* means body. In Tibet, however, it came to mean the emanation of an advanced Buddhist master who chooses to continue to incarnate for the benefit of others.

Tummo. (Tib.) An advanced Vajrayana practice for combining bliss and emptiness which produces heat as a by product. This is one of the Six Yogas of Naropa.

Two accumulations. (Tib. *shogs nyis*) The accumulation of merit with concepts and the accumulation of wisdom beyond concepts.

Two obscurations. There are two categories of obscurations or defilements that cover one's buddha nature: the defilement of conflicting emotions (see *five poisons & afflictive obscurations*) and the defilement of latent tendencies or sometimes called the obscuration of dualistic perception, or the intellectual/cognitive obscurations (see *cognitive obscurations*). The first category prevents sentient beings from freeing themselves from samsara, while the second prevents them from gaining accurate knowledge and realising truth.

Two truths. Relative truth and ultimate truth. Relative truth describes the superficial and apparent mode of all things. Ultimate truth describes the true and unmistaken mode of all things. These two are described differently in the different schools, each progressively deeper leading closer to the way things are.

Vajra. (Tib. *dorje*) Usually translated "diamond like." This may be an implement held in the hand during certain Vajrayana ceremonies, or it can refer to a quality which is so pure and so enduring that it is like a diamond.

Vajra posture. This refers to the full-lotus posture in which the legs are interlocked. When one leg is placed before the other as many Westerners sit it is called the half-lotus posture.

Vajradhara. (Tib. *Dorje Chang*) "Holder of the vajra." *Vajra* means indestructible and *dhara* means holding, embracing or inseparable. The central figure in the Kagyu refuge tree, and indicating the transmission of the close lineage of the Mahamudra teachings to Tilopa. Vajradhara symbolizes the primordial wisdom of the dharmakaya and wears the ornaments of the sambhogakaya Buddha, symbolizing its richness.

Vajravarahi. (Tib. *Dorje Phagmo*) A dakini who is the consort of Chakrasamvara. She is the main yidam of the Kagyu lineage and the embodiment of wisdom.

Vajrayogini. (Tib. *Dorje Palmo*) A semi-wrathful yidam. Female.

Vajrayana. (Tib. *dorje tek pa*) Literally, "diamond-like" or "indestructible capacity." *Vajra* here refers to method, so you can say the method yana. There are three major traditions of Buddhism (Hinayana, Mahayana, Vajrayana) The Vajrayana is based on the tantras and emphasizes the clarity aspect of phenomena. A practitioner of the method of taking the result as the path.

View, meditation, and action. (Tib. *ta ba gom pa yodpa*) The philosophical orientation, the act of growing accustomed to that – usually in sitting practice, and the implementation of that insight during the activities of daily life. Each of the three vehicles has its particular definition of view, meditation and action.

Vipashyana meditation. (Tib. *lha tong*) Sanskrit for "insight meditation." This meditation develops insight into the nature of reality (Skt. *dharmata*). One of the two main aspects of meditation practice, the other being Shamatha.

Wheel of dharma. (Skt. *dharmachakra*) The Buddha's teachings correspond to three levels which very briefly are: the first turning was the teachings on the four noble truths and the teaching of the egolessness of person; the second turning was the teachings on emptiness and the emptiness of phenomena; the third turning was the teachings on luminosity and buddha nature.

Whispered lineage. Instructions that concern emptiness and that come from jnana yoga dakinis.

Yana. Means capacity. There are three yanas, narrow, (Hinayana) great (Mahayana) and indestructible (Vajrayana).

Yidam. (Tib.) *Yi* means mind and *dam* means pure, or *yi* means your mind and *dam* means inseparable. The yidam represents the practitioner's awakened nature or pure appearance. A tantric deity that embodies qualities of buddhahood and is practiced in the Vajrayana. Also called a tutelary deity.

Yidam meditation. (Tib.) Yidam meditation is the Vajrayana practice that uses the visualization of a yidam.

Yoga. "Natural condition." A person who practices this is called a *yogi,* characterized by leaving everything natural, just as it is, e.g. not washing or cutting your hair and nails etc. A female practitioner is called a *yogini.*

Yogatantra. (Tib. *naljor gyi gyu*) Literally, "union tantra" and refers to a tantra that places emphasis on internal meditations.

Yogi. (Tib *nal yor pa*) Tantric practitioner.

Yogini. (Tib *nal yor ma*) Female tantric practitioner.

Glossary of Tibetan Terms

Pronounced	Transliterated	English
bardo	bar do	intermed. stage
bya ba gyu	bya ba'i rgyud	kriya tantra
cha ja chen po	phyag rgya chen po	Mahamudra
chang chup sem pa	byang chub sems dpa'	bodhisattva
chang chup sems	byang chub kyi sems	bodhichitta
che rim	bskyed rim	develop. stage
chin kor	dkyil 'khor	mandala
chö	chos	dharma
chö kyi wangs	chos dbyings	dharmadhatu
da po	mkha' 'gro	daka
do	mdo	sutra
dorje	rdo rje	vajra
dorje gur	rdo rje gur?	dohas
dorje tek pa	rdo rje theg pa	Vajrayana
drup chen	grub thob chen po	mahasiddha
dzog rim	rdzogs rim	completion
grong 'jug	phowa	ejection consc.
gur		doha
gyu lu	sgyu lus	illusory body
gyu	rgyud	tantra
gyu ma chen mo		Mahamaya trantra
Kagyu	bka' brgyud	Kagyu
kal pa	bskal pa	kalpa
khandra	mkha' gro ma	dakini

khyung	khyung	garuda
kon chok sum	dkon mchog gsum	three jewels
kor wa	'khor ba	samsara
ku sum	sku gsum	kayas, three
kye dorje	kye' rdo rje	Hevajra tantra
lama	bla ma	guru
lay	las	karma
lung	lung	ritual reading
mi lam	rmi lam	dream practice
mtha' bzhi		four empowerments
na bor pa	rnal 'byor pa	yogini
na ro cho drug	na ro chos drug	six yogas, Naropa
nam tar	rnam thar	biography
nsl jot ls ns mr pay ju	rnal 'byor bla na med pa'i	Anuttarayoga
nya ngen lay day pa		nirvana
nyon mongs		klesha
pan di ta	pan di ta	pandita
parol tu chinpa	pha rol tu phyin pan	paramita
phowa	'pho ba / grong 'jug	ejection of consc.
pung pa	phung po	skandha
rinpoche	rin po che	incarnate lama
sang pa dus pa	gsang ba 'dus	Guhyasamaja
she rab	shes rab	prajna
srang		gold
tan pa hyui dar		later translation school
tan pur nga dar		early translation school
thangka	thang ka	scroll painting
tong pa nyi	stong pa nyid	shunyata
torma	gtor ma	ritual cake
tri	'khrid	practice instuct. tsa way
lama	rtsa bai bla ma	root lama
tummo	gtum mo	subtle heat
wong	dbang bsku	empowerment
yeshe	ye shes	wisdom
yidam	yi dam	meditational deity

Bibliography

The All-Accomplishing Melody by Khyentse Rinpoche. This prayer has not been previously translated into English except for here.

Chanting the Names of Manjushri (Skt. *Manjushri Nama Sangiti*). Translated by Alex Wayman: Shambhala, Boston, 1985. This Text is probably the most revered and recited tantric text among all the Tibetan Buddhist sects.

The Life and Teachings of Naropa. Translated by Herbert Guenther: Oxford, London, University Press, 1963. Also *Illusion's Game, The Life and Teachings of Naropa* by Chogyam Trungpa Rinpoche: Shambhala, Boston, 1994.

The Life of Marpa the Translator. Translated by the Nalanda Translation Committee: Shambhala, Boston, 1986.

The LIfe of Milarepa. Translated by Lobsang Lhalungpa: Granada Publishing, London, 1979.

The Rain of Wisdom. Translated by the Nalanda Translation Committee: Shambhala, Boston, 1980.

The Spiritual Songs of Saraha. Translated by Edward Conze in *Buddhist Texts Through the Ages*: Bruno Cassierer, Oxford, 1954.

Index

A Long Life Prayer for the Glorious Lama, Scholar and Siddha

Thrangu Tulku, Karma Lodro Lungrik Maway Senge

The Youthful Vitality of Immortal Nectar

In Praise of Amitayus

OM SWASTI DZI WEN TU

The dharmakaya, free of elaboration is ever stable and never destroyed.
Amitayus, your speech is the melodious sound of the nada,
the invincible vajra.
Through an enlightened mind that sees all possible phenomena
Perfect Guide, you accomplish all goodness.

In Praise of Thrangu Rinpoche

From the golden age arose a new mansion of clouds
poised in the depth of space;
May you remain for a long, long time.
Creating festive occasions for beings to increase their merit.
May you remain for a long, long time.
Through the blooming, full lotus of your flawless knowledge,
Your writings are suffused with great kindness and compassion.
Through limitless abilities, you satisfy
a multitude of beings seeking liberation.
Guide of beings, may your life be long.
Through explaining the Dharma, you release beings
from the tangled net of ignorance and confusion
In debate, you defeat the opponents' bold stance.
Our minds are carried away with joy by the nature of your writings.
You of genuine and powerful speech, may your life be long.
Rising from the jeweled ocean of your immeasurable merit,
the white moon, clear mandala of your wisdom.
Pours forth nectar that is the light of your activity.
Lion of speech, teaching scripture and reasoning, may your life be long.

The Dedication

By churning an ocean of milk with good intentions,
These words of aspiration-a white lotus garland-come to the surface
Protector, through the merit of offering this
to all the buddhas and bodhisattvas.
May the benefit of your life last for hundreds of aeons.
Glorious Lama, through the power of the truth of the Victorious One.
Amitayus, and the power of a good connection with this sincere,
pure intention.
May your life remain stable until the end of the world.
May the vitality of all the four, perfectly flourish.
(Dharma, wealth, enjoyment, and liberation).

This prayer was requested by the one responsible for Nenang Monastery,
Lama Tsewang Tashi, who offered representations of the Buddha's body,
speech, and mind, and was written by the
XVIIth Karmapa, Urgyen Trinley Dorje
during a fine waxing moon of Saga Dawa.
SHUBHAM.

May it be a cause for virtue.

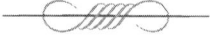

Care of Dharma Books

Dharma books contain the teachings of the Buddha; they have the power to protect against lower rebirth and to point the way to Liberation. Therefore, they should be treated with respect, kept off the floor and places where people sit or walk, and not stepped over. They should be covered or protected for transporting and kept in a high, clean place separate from more "ordinary" things. If it is necessary to dispose of Dharma materials, they should be burned with care and awareness rather than thrown in the trash. When burning Dharma texts, it is considered skilful to first recite a prayer or mantra, such as OM, AH, HUNG. Then you can visualize the letters of the text (to be burned) being absorbed into the AH, and the AH being aborbed into you. After that you can burn the texts.

These considerations may be also kept in mind for Dharma artwork, as well as the written teachings and artwork of other religions.